Ancestral Geographies of the Neolithic

Ancestral Geographies of the Neolithic is a vivid portrait of life in the small, dispersed communities of Neolithic Britain. Focussing in on the landscape and monuments of the fourth millennium BC, Mark Edmonds provides a dramatic, colourful interpretation of how these prehistoric peoples understood the world in which they lived.

Central to this study is the idea that communities of the time may have thought about the land, and about themselves, in ways very different to those we take for granted today. Theirs was a world shaped by kinship, ancestry and various forms of affiliation. It was a world in which the dead were a powerful presence, and where distant times and places held a particular fascination. Many of these themes were brought into sharpest focus during periodic gatherings at the monumental enclosures and tombs that appear in our record for the first time, where communities engaged in ancestral rites, exchange and other forms of ceremonial. It was through both routine and ritual experience that dispersed and fragmented communities acknowledged their ties to the land, to the past and to each other.

Ancestral Geographies of the Neolithic will provide invaluable insights into later prehistory to students of archaeology and landscape history, and all those interested in how prehistoric landscapes were inhabited.

Mark Edmonds is a senior lecturer in landscape archaeology at the University of Sheffield. He is the author of *Stone Tools and Society*.

Ancestral Geographies of the Neolithic

Landscape, monuments and memory

Mark Edmonds

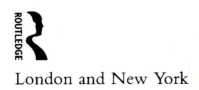

London and New York

Item Number

16569

First published 1999
by Routledge
11 New Fetter Lane, London EC4P 4EE

Transferred to Digital Printing 2003

Simultaneously published in the USA and Canada
by Routledge
29 West 35th Street, New York, NY 10001

© 1999 Mark Edmonds

Typeset in Bembo by
J&L Composition Ltd, Filey, North Yorkshire

All rights reserved. No part of this book may be reprinted or reproduced
or utilised in any form or by any electronic, mechanical, or other means,
now known or hereafter invented, including photocopying and recording,
or in any information storage or retrieval system, without permission in
writing from the publishers.

British Library Cataloguing in Publication Data
A catalogue record for this book is available from the British Library

Library of Congress Cataloging in Publication Data
Edmonds, M. R. (Mark R.)
  Ancestral geographies of the Neolithic: landscape, monuments and
  memory/Mark Edmonds
  p. cm.
  Includes bibliographical references and index.
  1. Neolithic period – Great Britain. 2. Earthworks (Archaeology) –
  Great Britain. 3. Human ecology – Great Britain. 4. Landscape
  assessment – Great Britain. 5. Great Britain – Antiquities.
  I. Title
  GN776.22.G7E33   1999
  936.1–dc21   98–36461
                                                            CIP

ISBN 0–415–07677–3 (HB)
ISBN 0–415–20432–1 (PB)

Printed and bound by Antony Rowe Ltd, Eastbourne

Contents

List of illustrations   vi
Preface   ix

1   Settings and scenes   1

2   Origins   11

3   Ancestral geographies   15

4   Keeping to the path   32

5   Working stone   36

6   A gift from the ancestors   51

7   The living and the dead   56

8   Attending to the dead   75

9   A time and a place for enclosure   80

10 Drawing the line   106

11 Arenas of value   110

12 The pattern of things   130

13 Changes in the land   134

14 Post excavation   152

Postscript   155
Bibliography   163
Index   169

Illustrations

1   Hambledon Hill, Dorset   2
2   Coppiced woodland   14
3   Earlier Neolithic hammerstone, blades, scrapers, fabricators
    and single piece sickles   17
4   Flaked and ground axes of flint and stone   19
5   Earlier Neolithic pottery   20
6   Coppiced woodland   22
7   The Sweet Track, Somerset Levels   25
8   Stone   35
9   Plans of earlier Neolithic mines in southern Britain   41
10 Shafts and galleries from three mines in Sussex. A: Blackpatch;
    B: Harrow Hill; C: Cissbury   43
11 Earlier Neolithic mine at Harrow Hill (Sussex) under
    excavation   45
12 Surface exposure of axe-making debris on an old working
    floor   46
13 A stone axe quarry in the central Lakeland fells   47
14 Hands holding stone   48
15 Bones and skull   55
16 The structural sequence at Wayland's Smithy, Oxfordshire   57
17 Facade at Wayland's Smithy   58
18 Mortuary and facade structures at a. Nutbane; b. Haddenham.
    c. Mortuary deposits at Fussell's Lodge   60
19 Earlier Neolithic mortuary sites. a. Facade and burial chambers
    at West Kennet. b. Wayland's Smithy. c. Willerby wold.
    d. Fussell's Lodge. e. Streethouse   62
20 a. South Street, Wiltshire. b. Beckhampton Road, Wiltshire   64
21 Tombs in the Derbyshire Peak District
    a. Long barrow with superimposed round barrow at Perryfoot.
    b. Long barrow with superimposed round barrow at
    Longstone Moor. c. Five Wells chambered barrow. d. Green
    Low chambered barrow. e. Minninglow. f. Chambered bank
    barrow at Long Low   66

22	Outline plan of the great barrow and surrounding enclosure at Duggleby Howe, Yorkshire	69
23	Plan of the double-ditched barrow at Barrow Hills, constructed on the margins of a causewayed enclosure near Abingdon	71
24	Whitegrounds, Yorkshire	72
25	Articulated body of a man in the entrance to the north chamber of Hazelton long cairn, Gloucestershire	74
26	a. Rybury. b. Haddenham	79
27	Knap Hill, Wiltshire	81
28	Knap Hill from the ground	82
29	Whitesheet Hill, Wiltshire	84
30	Windmill Hill, Wiltshire	86
31	Aerial photograph of Long Meg and her Daughters (Cumbria)	87
32	The stone-banked enclosure at Gardom's Edge, Derbyshire	88
33	Causewayed ditch at Hambledon Hill	90
34	Land-use potentials around four enclosures	91
35	The relationship between the enclosure and earlier longhouses at Langweiller 8	94
36	Longhouses and enclosure at Darion, Belgium	96
37	The two phases of enclosure at Sarup, Denmark	97
38	a. The Trundle, Sussex. b. Whitehawk, Sussex	100
39	Crickley Hill, Gloucestershire: Phase 1b	102
40	a. Briar Hill, Northamptonshire. b. Robin Hood's Ball, Wiltshire	103
41	a. Great Wilbraham. b. Knap Hill	109
42	Enclosure, cursus and predominantly later cropmarks at Etton, Cambridgeshire	111
43	Primary ditch deposits at Etton	112
44	Haddenham, Cambridgeshire	114
45	Skull in ditch at Hambledon Hill	116
46	a. Etton. b. Upton. c. Uffington. d. Melbourn. e. Roughton	118
47	Skull in ditch at Maiden Castle, Dorset	119
48	a. Coombe Hill. b. Orsett. c. Great Wilbraham	120
49	a. Association of human remains with ditchworks at Offham. b. Burial from Offham. c. Burial from Staines	122
50	a. Southwick. b. Barholm. c. Northborough	123
51	Animal bone in the ditch of Windmill Hill	124
52	A small axe from the Lake District deposited in a pit at Etton, near Peterborough	125
53	Cornish ground stone axe and pot deposited at Hambledon Hill, Dorset	126
54	a. Windmill Hill. b. Melbourn. c. Briar Hill. d. Hambledon Hill	133
55	Body in ditch at Hambledon Hill, Dorset	135
56	Hambledon Hill, Dorset	136

57   The Stepleton enclosure at Hambledon Hill   139
58   Maiden Castle, Dorset, showing the position of the long
       mound in relation to the enclosure   140
59   Crickley Hill, Gloucestershire: Phase 1d   142
60   Distribution of arrowheads around one of the entrances at
       Crickley Hill, Gloucestershire   143
61   Plan of the Dorset cursus   146
62   Detail of the monument complex at Dorchester-on-Thames,
       Oxfordshire   147
63   Abingdon, Oxfordshire   148
64   The Trundle, Sussex   151

Preface

This book has taken quite a while to complete. It began with an article on earlier Neolithic causewayed enclosures that I wrote in the late 1980s. In it I tried to compress everything that I felt I had to say about these enigmatic monuments, reviewing evidence and the arguments of others. The result was turgid and impenetrable; I can't look at it now.

A few years after the article was submitted, I began to think about developing some of its themes in a more extended discussion. At that stage, I planned to write a rather conventional study, an overtly analytical work which reviewed the character and chronology of enclosures in southern Britain. Libraries were excavated for references and the book began to take some sort of shape; chapters on the history of interpretation, on traditions of construction and on the landscape setting of enclosures in different regions. Much of the text seemed rather lifeless, but I had produced about forty to fifty thousand words, and was reluctant to scrap the files and start again. Fortunately, fate intervened. We were burgled twice in three days and I lost the lot. Along with all the usual appliances and CDs, the burglar made off with a briefcase containing all the back-up files and a novel by Peter Ackroyd. If they have tried to read any of the text, they have probably been punished enough.

Given the chance to start again, I decided to approach the book in a different way. I began to realise that the difficulties I had been having were as much a problem of writing as they were a problem with the evidence. The arguments were detached. On the one hand, there was abstract discussion of the relationship between material tradition and social life, of the importance of ritual and of the ways in which institutions might be sustained through people's practice. On the other, there was the evidence itself, the products of survey, excavation and argument accumulated over more than a century. The two sides seemed unconnected; theoretical insights and material details kept missing each other.

There were, of course, good reasons for this. The evidence is grey on many issues and this often encourages abstraction. However, the problem was more basic than that. The book, like many others, missed both the humanity and the materiality of the times and places that I was interested in. It failed to capture any sense of what it may have been to inhabit what we call the earlier

Neolithic, to participate in the building and use of monuments or to follow the customary pattern of daily and seasonal routines. The past constructed on the page was peopled either by dull archetypes who spent their lives chasing and producing food, or automata, blindly reproducing abstracted and simplistic symbolic codes. At least some of the jargon was simply rhetoric, wielded as 'science' sometimes is, to confer a sense of authority on thin descriptions of the material.

This situation is to some extent inevitable. The past is dead and we cannot reconstruct it 'as it was'. There is always a gap. It was the recognition of that gap and its intellectual consequences that led David Clarke to suggest nearly thirty years ago that archaeology had lost its innocence. Since then, we also seem to have lost our nerve. We have lost sight of the fact that, for all of our technique and our rhetoric to the contrary, the study of the past is an act of the imagination, bound by convention and by evidence, but creative nonetheless.

In what follows, I have tried to acknowledge this fact of our practice in the structure of the book itself. A good deal of the text deals with questions of process and change over time. Much as others have done, I have tried to establish something of the character of life at the time, and have asked how these conditions contributed to the reproduction of the social world. 'Reproduction' here means both the maintenance and reworking of the social categories and relations that are bound up in particular ways of living. That interest stems from the fact that the ideas and institutions that people recognise do not exist simply in the abstract: they are part of the fabric of practical life and it is through the reworking of practice that they are often changed. Inculcated by instruction, observation and bodily experience, they are also thoroughly historical. Just how these processes may have worked is something that we often seem to miss in our writing. Sometimes it is a problem of scale, sometimes a problem of emphasis. We create grand narratives, or talk in the abstract about relations between material tradition and social life. What often gets lost is any sense of how particular conditions were inhabited, how tasks, places and performances contributed to the interplay of relations between people and to social change.

It is with these problems in mind that I have experimented a little with the normal conventions of much archaeological writing. I have tried to make the text less determined and more open, and that is why I have decided against the use of in-text references. These have their place, but they can also weigh down a text, and they can certainly make it too exclusive. I have also tried to avoid a long, abstracted theoretical preamble for much the same reasons. In addition, the book includes a series of short, narrative texts. These stories do not bridge the gap between present and past any more than the rest of the book does. However, I hope that they go some way towards catching how some of the places and concepts that we study may have been understood and carried forward by people at the time.

Unless otherwise stated, the photographs and illustrations in this book are the work of the author. The only exceptions are the composite aerial photographs of enclosures that occur before chapters 9, 11 and 13. These are reproduced with the permission of the Cambridge Library for Aerial Photography.

This book is also a product of discussions and conversations with many friends. Over the past few years, I have been lucky enough to exchange ideas and arguments with a variety of people, many of whom, I am sure, will have difficulties with some or all of what follows. At Sheffield, I have gained much from arguments shared with John Moreland, Paul Halstead, Glynis Jones, John Barrett and Mike Parker Pearson. People on the landscape MA, particularly Mel Giles, Danny Hind and Graham Robbins, have also had a significant impact on my way of thinking and writing. The book would have been very different without them. Jacinta and Dagmar know the enormous debt I owe to them. Outside Sheffield, there are many others, Barbara Bender, Richard Bradley, Francis Pryor and Maisie Taylor, Colin Richards and Julian Thomas among them. I thank them for the pleasure of working together and for their encouragement. Barbara deserves particular thanks for her support and enthusiasm and for her help with the dialogue. Several paragraphs in chapter 1 are reproduced from an article that we wrote some time ago on the rituals of routine practice.

Two people stand out. I began thinking about this book while working in Cambridge. There I was fortunate enough to get to know Chris Evans and Marie-Louise Stig Sørenson. Conversations about archaeology and other things set much of the course that this book has taken. Indeed, at one point Chris and I discussed working together on something along similar lines. Reading what follows, some might feel it's a shame that we didn't. In the hope that I've made at least some good use of that time, I dedicate the book to them.

> . . . the act of approaching a given moment of experience involves both scrutiny (closeness) and the capacity to connect (distance). The movement of writing resembles that of a shuttle on a loom: repeatedly it approaches and withdraws, closes in and takes its distance. Unlike a shuttle, however, it is not fixed to a static frame. As the movement of writing repeats itself, its intimacy with the experience increases. Finally, if one is fortunate, meaning is the fruit of this intimacy.
>
> (John Berger, *Pig Earth*, 1982)

Mark Edmonds
Sheffield, 1998

1 Settings and scenes

Landscape and history

Hambledon Hill. A chalk dome with three great spurs that rises between Child Okeford and Shroton in Dorset. Cretaceous. Marine life made geology by pressure and time. Crows wheel above slopes that shift in and out of focus, artefacts of mist and changes in the light. Giant furrows fold back upon the rise and on each other, sinuous earthworks that follow the contour, turning up in places to cross the ridge. Drawn along these lines, the eye is pulled, like centuries of soil, down folds and slopes to lower ground, to the Vale of Blackmoor and Cranborne Chase. The view is a familiar one. It is a patchwork of fields and hedgerows, of hamlets, villages and more isolated farms. Ash trees caught in hedges hold the line of old boundaries in their boughs. Beech stands turn to copper and bronze each autumn, catching fire in the low sun of late afternoon. There is even a yew wood, dark and dense against the green. Some consider the wood to be haunted. Ghosts walk in stories that resonate around the hill, only to be lost with increasing distance. The stories are local; tethered to the land.

Like the earthworks on the hilltop, much of this scene appears timeless. For Thomas Hardy, who stumbled in the mists on Hambledon in the 1890s, the land was a constant. The Wessex he created was an old country, one in which '. . . the busy outsider's ancient times are only old: his old times are still new; his present is futurity.' The land had stability and depth and this seemed condensed in the prehistoric monuments that lay scatttered across its surface: barrows, stone circles and great chalk banks; ruins already scarred by collectors and by scientific interest. These features are a powerful presence in his novels. They lend a mythic weight to the human stories that he tells, hinting that the forces driving his protagonists are just as old and changeless. At times it is as if the land itself determines human nature and their destiny.

Reworked in more recent writing and through landscape portraiture, this nostalgic image of an almost timeless rural world remains powerful. The land is something to gaze upon, to appeal to and to own. A constant in the England of advertising and in the empty rhetoric of certain politicians, it remains an icon. Used to sell everything from butter to foreign policy, it is

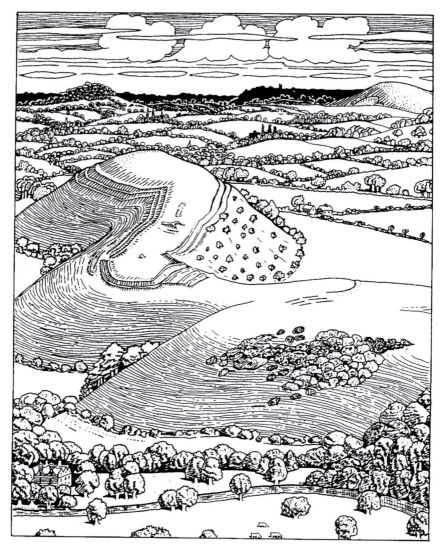

Figure 1 Hambledon Hill, Dorset. (After Heywood Sumner.)

stable and reassuring, a foundation for some of our origin myths of national identity. Looked at more closely, the scene has a past which cuts against the grain of those myths. It is a surface inhabited over millennia, variously worked and changed by people. Lines of hawthorn and ash follow the edges of medieval tracks and fields, enclosing land where old furrows survive as soil marks. Other hedges are the imprint of more recent hands, boundaries set in the last two centuries. There are other traces too. Seen from the air, the land is etched with the marks of prehistory: places of settlement and ceremonial and of dead long since forgotten; sites revealed when the plough brings its varied crop of pottery and stone to the surface.

Time and change are also inscribed on the hill itself; a duration acknowledged in Heywood Sumners' plan from 1911. Beneath the trig point that ties it to the geometry of the modern are older and more varied features. There are fields and marl pits only a few centuries old, evidence for grazing and cultivation that continue to this day. Anglo-Saxon burials have also been identified. Bodies were laid to rest in older banks that looked down upon a land where both kinship and kingship were important concerns. Older still are the earthworks of an Iron Age hill-fort, turf-covered ramparts that once were white. Another, Hod Hill, lies on an adjacent crest. Developed in the centuries around the Roman occupation, the hill-fort dominated the skylines and the consciousness of those who lived and worked on lower ground. Associated with the *Durotriges*, it was a place of occupation and of periodic gatherings, a statement cut deep into the chalk. Softened now by a mantle of grass, it has remained a point of reference. Even now, the parish boundary between Child Okeford and Shroton runs through the hill-fort and along the eastern inner rampart. The place is also remembered for its use in the 'pitchfork rebellion', when local relations were recast by the upheavals of the Civil War.

The line goes further. The 'old camp' reoccupied by the Clubmen of 1645 was itself a reworking of the hill. Those who lived and assembled during the Iron Age acknowledged older features and other pasts. There are Bronze Age barrows on the crest, perhaps even settlement and cultivation, and there are older barrows still; two earlier Neolithic long mounds, respected as people cut ditches or set platforms in the chalk. These mounds were older than a hundred generations by the time the first ramparts were raised, and yet they were recognised, given space within the boundaries and in the flow of later life across the hill. A similar respect was shown to the earthworks of enclosures as old as these mounds, low banks and ditches that crown the hill and its spurs. Diminutive now and best seen in low light, the line of these older features seems to have inspired the position of some of the later earthworks.

The hill has been used and understood in many ways over time. It has been at the centre and on the margins of things, a place of gatherings and burial, of settlement, cultivation and bold gestures. Despite the stability it seems to embody, it is not a constant. The same can be said of the land that falls away on every side. Permanent though they seem to us, the features that we cherish today are products of social and political geographies very different from our own. We don't have to go that far back. Many hedgerows belong to a time when land once held as common was consolidated in the hands of a few by piecemeal and parliamentary enclosure. Estates that cash-cropped sheep on old commons and fields recast traditional patterns of residence and labour. There was a break with older, customary geographies, one which did not serve the interests of all. Writing in Northamptonshire in the eighteenth century, John Clare demonstrated that many of these changes were far from uncontested. For him, as for those who challenged new rents or worked to breach new hedges and ditches, enclosure changed the land.

> There once were lanes in nature's freedom dropt,
> There once were paths that every valley wound –
> Inclosure came, and every path was stopt;
> Each tyrant fix'd his sign where paths were found,
> To hint a trespass now who cross'd the ground:
> Justice is made to speak as they command;
> The high road now must be each stinted bound:
> Inclosure, thou'rt a curse upon the land,
> and tasteless was the wretch who thy existence plann'd.

Clare romanticised the past that came before enclosure. He said little of the inheritance of older ways of living and working or of older tensions: seigneural relations; duties to markets, state and church; or the moral and obligatory ties that stretched back and forth between communities. It was enough that some were threatened. Yet it is a quality of his poetry that it highlights the local, everyday, consequences of developments usually discussed at a more general scale. What he tells us is that the land was not a static backdrop to the events and processes of his time. It lay at the heart of social life. Inhabited and reworked at both local and regional scales, it was an artefact of history. His writing is also important in another way. Passionate and situated, it clashes with many contemporary images of landscape found in the paintings and literature commissioned by members of 'polite' society. It reminds us that ways of living through and even thinking about landscape were as political as they were practical.

Approaching Neolithic monuments

So far as we know, Clare never visited Hambledon, yet his observations take us to the heart of what makes the hill and places like it so remarkable. Often difficult to recognise and always difficult to comprehend, the accumulated earthworks that survive are both the medium and the outcome of relations between people in the past. They were created in step with the understandings that people had of their worlds, of who they were and of their relations with others: personal, familial, communal, political; identities and authorities bound up in the practical facts of living and in moments of performance or observance. The hill tells us something else as well. Patterns in the playing out of earthworks suggest that these monuments were often objects of thought, caught up in the pattern and purpose of people's lives long after they were constructed. What they may have meant to much later generations is not always clear. Traces of heroic pasts, fashioned in myth to serve particular interests. Part of the land itself, acknowledged only in passing and in moments of reflection. Forgotten altogether, only to be rediscovered and accorded new values. Hambledon reminds us that the past was not a neat succession of periods, opening and closing like the chapters of a book, each one characterised by a distinctive set of traits. The playing out of relations between people involved the piecemeal inheritance, abandonment and rediscovery of the past as it appeared in their present.

That, of course, is easily said. It is easy to assert that material traditions – patterns of life and labour – are intimately bound up in the reproduction of the social world. It is rather more difficult to flesh out those ties, to chart their articulation, or to follow how they changed. Even when we study comparatively recent history, the task is far from easy. It is hard to capture the spirit of the time when the Clubmen gathered, or when rights of access sustained over generations were cut by new forms of ownership and new loyalties. These histories are complex, contradictory and close grained. They resist being grasped in any one account and are often obscured by the very concepts or scales of analysis that we use. More often than not history gives way to process; local currents of identity and authority are lost in the flow of grander narratives. These problems are compounded the further back in time that we go. As centuries become millennia, our evidence changes in character and in material detail. Familiar landmarks fade from view and it becomes all the more difficult to establish contexts and points of reference. Under these circumstances, the broadest processes often come to dominate accounts.

Nowhere is this problem more acute than in our attempts to 'make sense' of some of the earliest features on the hill. Conventionally assigned to the early fourth millennium BC, the long mounds and enclosures of the earlier Neolithic are traces of a world very different from today. We are certainly not the first to interpret that world, but it is customary nowadays to be quite circumspect. We talk of a time when people had begun to experiment with stock and crops, when ancestors were a powerful presence in the land, a time when life was bound to a seasonal wheel and to webs of kinship, descent and local renown. Yet for all of our disciplinary rigour and our technical accomplishment, it is a difficult world to capture; fragmentary and elusive.

Our difficulties with the earlier Neolithic in Britain stem from many sources. To begin with, the inception of the period shifts back and forth between models of indigenous development and colonisation during the later fifth and early fourth millennia. Debate has been made all the more complex by the lack of good radiocarbon dates for the horizon separating the Neolithic from its predecessor, the Mesolithic. Further problems arise because this transition also marks the meeting point between different traditions of enquiry. The two periods have generally been studied by different groups of scholars, each with their own perspectives and priorities. This division of labour has become so entrenched that we often seem to forget that the two periods are rationalisations, developed by us to make sense of our evidence.

This confusion has been compounded by the fact that our definitions of the term 'Neolithic' have been far from constant. Some use the term to talk of definitive traits such as farming, that are independent of time and space, others use it to denote a specific historical process, and it is not uncommon for people to shift back and forth between the two. Originally a label attached to a stage in a general evolutionary scheme, the passage of time saw the term come to denote a cultural phenomenon, marked by a distinctive repertoire of sites and artefacts, some of which have continental parallels. Talk of Neolithic cultures has, in its turn, given way to a view of the period as an economic entity, associated with a switch from hunting and gathering to food production. More recently still, interest has shifted towards a view of the period as a time that saw the development of new ways of thinking about land, people and even time itself.

What else do we commonly say about the earlier Neolithic? We bracket it with radiocarbon and talk of its persistence for about a thousand years. Dates are often imprecise, but it is common to draw a line between around 4000 and 3000 BC. We also talk about it as a time which saw changes in material traditions; the first appearance of pottery and the first widespread use of polished stone tools. Like domesticated plants and animals, these are common features in discussion. More often than not, we talk about the ceremonial monuments that appear in the early fourth millennium: long mounds associated with the remains of the dead and enclosures with interrupted and irregular ditches; mines, quarries or the long parallel banks of cursus monuments. Varied in character, chronology and distribution, these places are prominent in many accounts.

This fascination with monuments has taken many forms and it persists for many reasons. These are places that have endured. Although many have been eroded by time and the plough, there are still enough upstanding earthworks to catch the eye and the imagination. Many are also enigmatic. Their persistence confronts us with a sense of deep time; form and content revealing an otherness or difference that is always just beyond our grasp. Often associated with fragmentary human remains, with evidence for feasting and other forms of ceremonial, they hint at ways of living and thinking that jar with the present. Qualities once evoked by Hardy, these themes are now crucial to what are often casually dismissed as 'alternative' views. Yet there is more here than just a desire for difference, romanticism or nostalgia. The simple persistence of many of these monuments often reflects a considerable and protracted expenditure of effort. This in itself means little enough. Unmodified features can be accorded spiritual or historical significance, and this may have been important at the time. However, the character and scale of places like tombs and enclosures suggests that many occupied prominent positions in the social and symbolic landscapes of the early fourth millennium.

How do we understand these places? For some, long mounds and enclosures are an expression of a cultural change, a product of the arrival of new people and/or new ideas. On occasion, they have been seen as a direct consequence of the development of agriculture. For others, the scale of particular monuments has been read as an index of social complexity, investment of effort a reflection of the authority achieved or inherited by a few at the time. Recently, the focus has been at a more intimate scale, reflecting a concern with the changing meanings of these places and the events they witnessed. Here it is common to find a view of monuments as frames upon which social memories and values could be inscribed. Work on tombs has recognised that the ways people made sense of death lay at the heart of their ways of thinking about themselves and their relation to the world around them. Studies of other monuments have also acknowledged that in the earlier Neolithic, as elsewhere, ritual and public ceremonial was crucial to the reproduction of certain forms of authority. For many, the power of various rites was to some extent derived from their enactment within and around the monuments that we can still see today.

These ideas have taken research in many directions. There is now a rich and varied literature on the roles that monuments played in the earlier Neolithic, and on the character and significance of ceremonies conducted within their bounds. A lot of work has been done on long mounds and megaliths, on enclosures and ceremonial ways. We have explored acts of construction, offerings and rituals, and movement in and around the places of death, ancestry and initiation. Latterly, we have begun to trace the ways in which processions and formal patterns of movement link ritual sites across the landscape. In doing so, at least some of the lines drawn between orthodox and alternative perspectives have been eroded. Crucial to much recent research has been the idea that people do not think about their world in the abstract, or even gaze at it like some painting in a frame. Rather, they experience it physically. They move around, go in and out of places, they congregate and they disperse. They can go in certain directions but not others. They can go to certain monuments, but only when the time is right. Boundaries and pathways, places of secrecy or danger, formal and informal settings, backstage and frontstage and places in between all help to shape the world of ritual experience. Much of what happens in these times and places is constituted by the past, by real or invented tradition and by what is already there. Through what some have called a 'technology of memory', people absorb, reuse and rework the past through their physical encounter with particular monuments and performative or ritual events.

These shifts of perspective have been valuable, but our descriptions can still seem disappointingly thin. To say that the earlier Neolithic lasts about a thousand years is one thing. To talk of that time as a span of around forty to fifty generations is quite another. It suggests that at least some traditions were remarkably persistent and we should ask why that might be. Also, it reminds us that while monuments and ritual can be central to the ways in which societies remember, they are far from monolithic. Their meanings and their roles can change, just as they may vary from one setting to another. The fact that some were worked and reworked over centuries suggests that this is likely to have been the case.

There are other qualities to monuments that we sometimes miss. A great many accounts look only at their role in the reproduction of political hierarchies. There is a preoccupation with chiefs or regional elites, and rather less discussion of the broader social landscapes in which particular monuments were set. Questions of hierarchy are, of course, important. Forms of authority were present at most places and times and we need to understand how they were reproduced. But we should also consider those other themes that may have animated life in the past: categories based on family and kin affiliation, on gender, and on all the different grades of child- and adulthood. These identities are difficult to grasp, but many would have been brought into sharp relief during events at monuments. People's senses of who they were and what was expected of them would shape and be shaped by their participation in rituals going on around them. And this participation and understanding would not remain static. What could be done or said, where a person could or could not go, would change according to context and audience, as people got older, were initiated, became married or widowed.

This idea takes us beyond monuments themselves. Whilst acknowledging their power and the drama of ritual performance, we have to work between these settings and the landscapes of the everyday. Unless we explore the conditions under which people came together at important times and places, we cannot begin to understand the particular purposes they served. We cannot ask how rituals were woven into cycles of routine experience, and we miss how routine itself was caught up in social reproduction.

It is here that we encounter problems in both conventional and more avant-garde archaeological writing. Discussions of daily and seasonal life and of feast days and ritual are separated by changes in the questions we ask and the imposition of rigid divisions: Sacred and Profane; Ceremonial and Everyday; Public and Domestic. Brought into play in the study of sites and artefacts, these divisions are also mapped out across regions. We maintain a distinction between sacred landscapes and the secular spaces of settlement and subsistence. This imbalance can be traced in a contrast of writing. The times and places of overt ritual are often explored through a rich and subtle vocabulary. Memory and movement are brought into focus, as are people and artefacts, and ways of speaking and acting can seem highly charged. This is often justified, but discussions of living and working can seem quite stark by comparison. Abstracted models or mundane descriptions, they often seem to obscure the character and craft of daily and seasonal life. More often than not, we seem to imply that the landscape of routine is shaped solely by resource availability, risk and the practical constraints of topography. There is little discussion of the attitudes and values that were woven into daily and seasonal practice. Above all else, our accounts of settlement and subsistence are remarkably static. If monuments could change and vary, so could the land itself, either as a result or in spite of people's actions. This again is something rarely explored.

These distinctions say rather more about us than they do about people in the earlier Neolithic. We create, through our narratives, a division between sacred and secular. We assume that these spheres can be bracketed off from one another: on one side a ritual world full of symbolic meaning; on the other, a pragmatic, common-sense world of getting on with things and making a living. The irony is that even in our own lives, these rigid divisions are a chimera. Whilst there are times and places that we recognise through formal rituals, our everyday lives are bound up by routines that are themselves symbolic. The ways in which we use domestic space, take decisions and act as we work, shop or laze around; all are informed by values which go beyond simple questions of utility. There are, in all contexts, right ways, right times, right places and wrong ones. It is through learning the conventions and craft involved in 'going on' that we come to recognise some of the categories and divisions that animate our world. This is how we become socialised and how social relations are reproduced. The ritual and symbolism of everyday life may be less explicit or obvious than that of more formal, sacred times and places – it often appears to us as common sense, or part of human nature – but it is all the more powerful precisely because it is taken for granted. Placed beyond question for much of the time, the values caught up in routine life help to reaffirm some of the familiar landmarks of the social world.

Thought about in this way, there is no part of the landscape that is not mediated by people's understandings of their world. No landscape sits 'out there', waiting to be exploited. Landscapes are subjective, understood as much by ways of acting as by ways of seeing. They are part of a world that is conceptualised and inhabited: seen, smelt, touched, used and avoided in terms of people's histories, identities and understandings. As such, they are contexts in which people can also question, baulk, negotiate and disrupt. So, alongside the study of the more formal times and places, we need to ask how the pattern and tempo of day-to-day life in the earlier Neolithic acted as a medium through which ideas and values were taken on board. We need to understand how, under certain conditions, practical routines carried forward particular concepts of identity, community and authority. Once again, these ideas are easy to assert, and some might argue that a shift of focus is forced upon us by our evidence. The complex histories revealed at Neolithic monuments seem to invite a 'jeweller's eye' approach. By contrast, the traces of daily life can seem ephemeral, encouraging discussion at a more general level. Here we must be careful. There may be differences in the character of our evidence and in the scales at which it is resolved. In each case, however, we are dealing with traditions, ways of thinking and acting which can be followed across space and through time. We need to ask how those threads were woven if we are to have any chance of catching the purposes that each may have served.

That question takes us back to Hambledon. Despite the level of survival and a wealth of excavation, there is much we do not understand and even more we cannot know about the significance that this place held for communities in the fourth millennium. All we have are fragments. We assemble these in a world shaped by very different values and desires, and these, in their turn, shape the pasts that we write. Even so, the evidence is such that it may still be possible to trace some of the contours of the time. One thing at least is clear: any attempt to make sense of monuments like those on the hill must work at several scales. The characteristics of these places must feature prominently, as must the manner in which they changed over time. Also, the focus must be broader, following the more routine, dispersed traditions that curled round these enigmatic times and places. While there is much that will remain elusive, the sketches that follow try to catch something of what it was to inhabit what we call the earlier Neolithic.

2 Origins

The old man leant forward and spat into the fire. He took a twist of dried meat from the bag at his side and drew his shoulders in towards the heat; a little further from the snow outside.

'This is how it is.'

He leaned back into the easy squat he had held for much of the evening. Others sat close by, hands working back and forth unnoticed across hide and wood. Where the shadows met the wall, the older children listened absent mindedly, familiar with the path the tale would take.

'Our first world was the forest, but before the forest there was ice. There was no colour and no time, no smoke and no tracks. The land was barren.'

He gestured over his shoulder to the wind outside. The twist was still in his hand, forgotten in the telling.

'Then the great spirits came. They breathed on the ice and made camps across its surface. Sparks from their hearths flew up into the sky. When the night is clear, you can still see the pattern of their seasonal round. To follow the pattern is to honour the debt that we owe.'

The old man was on well-trodden ground. The story had been told many times before; by him and by others. He knew the shape and the grain of it; knew where to embellish and where to stay true.

'They melted the ice with their working and it was through the holes that the forest grew. Freed by the heat, the water became the great river, the source from which all others sprang and the flow to which they all return. If you walk down-stream and between two moons you will come to its bank. You cannot see the other side. Part of us belongs there. Part of us always returns to the water.'

As he talked, the old man dipped his fingers into the pot that sat close by. Water raised in the cup of his hand trickled back into the vessel, catching light from the fire as it fell. Brought in from the stream as hard as stone, the ice had soon melted in the warmth of the lodge. He went on.

'The land was rich. River and forest were heavy with game and the land gave gifts that needed no return. It looked after its own. It was into this world that the old ones came, the first born; children of the trees and of the waters. The first of our line. The old ones moved easily through the woods. Paths opened before them of their own accord. Some took the form of the Bear or the Eagle as they went, others the Deer or the Wolf. Though they still hear us when we call, that gift is lost to all but the Shaman. This is how it is.'

The children called out the names they had heard since birth, carried along with the tale as it ranged across familiar hills and clearings. Two of the older boys lost interest and turned to flick twigs at the early calf tethered to the wall.

'As they moved across the land, the first born called down bolts of fire to clear the ground for their camps. Their steps made the paths that we tread, their middens the hills that rise on the far side of the river. As they went, they left signs for us to follow. Their arrows fell to earth and took root. Even now, you can see them in the tall, straight stands near where the good stone lies. Their spirits are strong there. Be careful. There are other spirits too, ones that will steal your birth cords from the river and make you lose your way. Once that happens, you are lost. You will never join the company of the ancestors.'

The old man paused and chewed the twist of bitter meat. He was approaching the place in the tale that always captured the children. The pause gave them time to see where they were going. Clearing his throat, he began again, arriving at the time when paths began to cross too often, when bad blood ran between the first clans. The bodies of those who had fallen in the fighting could still be traced in the land around them; in water, earth and stone. He recited the names, putting each one in its place. Warming to the tale and embroidering as he went, he spoke of a rock many days to the north, where the land was white with bones. Embedded in the rock was an axe that stood three times the height of a man. Perhaps they would see it one day. At a flourish of his hand, the children gazed up to the rafters and on through the gap where the smoke was drawn by the wind. This was the axe that had felled the wild bull with fire in his eyes. The rock was all that remained of his skull.

'It was a bitter feud. You can hear its echoes among the clans today. But when the bull's throat was cut, his blood spilled back into the earth and cattle sprang up where it fell. Tamed by his death, they were docile and easily led. From their first milk sprang the seed corn for the crops that grow in many gardens. This is their gift and our inheritance. This is how it is.'

The tale moved on. The old man remembered kin who had followed herds in earlier times, tracing the lines that joined their hearths. Some kept pace with him, while others wandered into different stories and to discussion of the snow outside. Horizons had shrunk with the cold, and there was talk of when the ancestors would bring the land to life again.

Sat to one side, the old man's daughter pushed the hide she had been scraping over her feet. Turning from the task, she pulled a core and hammer from the bag at her shoulder and struck a long flake. She held the hammer between forefinger and thumb as lightly as she might have held an egg too precious to drop. Her grip was soft yet confident. Without thinking, she let the hammer fall on the flint, just in from the edge, just above the ridge. There was a satisfying ring as a second thin blade came away from the core; a hiss as it shot to the ground between her knees. Selecting the straightest of the two, she turned back to the hide and began to cut. It would take four days. The hide was as stiff and reluctant as it had ever been, but it would soften in time. The boots would keep her warm when she gathered windfalls for the fire.

Figure 2

3   Ancestral geographies

The erosion of peat is transforming the Cambridgeshire fens. Driven by ever more intensive drainage and cultivation, the rich dark earth has been lost in many places. The wind drives across the open ground, carrying drifts of soil across roads and under doors. Few hedgerows remain to check its migration. Each year, the peat grows thinner. The flat black wash is scratched away, revealing an impasto surface of more varied form and colour, the yellows and browns of sand and gravel, the greys and blues of chalky marl. Long protected by the peat, this landscape is diverse. There are river channels and low valleys, flood plains and gravel terraces; meanders, promontories and drier 'uplands'. Exposed now to the threat of dessication, much of this land has not been seen or worked for more than three thousand years.

Erosion and aerial reconnaisance reveal a wealth of evidence for prehistoric activity in this region. There are fields and settlements, houses, ditches and the rough grids of pasture and arable. There are surface scatters of flint, much of it worked and burnt, on promontories or in the bends of rivers, across droveways, camps or barrows. And where water and peat still work together, there are timber trackways and platforms running out from the edges of diverse Fens. There is a long duration in this evidence. Stretching in places from the Mesolithic to the Iron Age, it spans ten thousand years and over four hundred generations.

There are patterns in the palimpsest. Dispersed across this surface and often appearing as points within later spreads are traces of what we recognise as the earlier Neolithic, perhaps a thousand years and over forty generations. Stone scatters, tombs and larger monuments; relict pollen and preserved timber or bone. At Isleham, meanders and gentle slopes mark the line of what we know as the Snail Valley. Emerging from beneath the peat, a relict river channel can now be traced upon the surface, a watercourse that has not run for millennia. Close inspection of this area has proved revealing. Scattered along the margins of the channel and spilling over its banks are the residues of activities that date to this time. Stone tools and waste are spread in varying densities, echoing patterns seen elsewhere. Captured in their forms are the outlines of tasks. There are scrapers made on the ends of flakes, their edges worn through use on leather and on other materials. There are simple blades used in preparing food and in other ways. Larger tools suggest the working of wood and there is evidence of flint knapping itself. Sealed in a shallow pit were the butt-ends of two polished flint axes, a well-worn hammerstone and flakes from the shaping and thinning of similar tools. Sherds of coarse pottery can be found in shallow features, or mixed into the deposits that tumble into the channel. Also present are the disarticulated bones of cattle, deer and people. Dispersed among this material are microliths and cores that reveal an older, Mesolithic, presence. Relict pollen speaks of clearings by the slow water's edge, of people living and working and people moving through.

What can places like the Snail Valley tell us about how people lived during the earlier Neolithic? What can we say about the values embodied in living and working across its surface? Our evidence is not easy to translate, but it suggests that the landscapes of the earlier Neolithic were dispersed and fragmented. This was a land inhabited by small communities, people for whom kinship, ancestry and local authority were vital concerns. Often no more than extended families, the pattern of their lives revolved around complex histories of movement and residence. This description says little in itself, but at once it jars with popular assumptions about the character and scale of life in southern Britain at the time. It is still a commonplace that the onset of the Neolithic saw people become sedentary, switching their allegiance from hunting and collecting to farming. Settling down is often emphasised, as is the role of food production, and the period marks the point in time where narratives evoke a rather homogenous impression of hamlets and fixed settlements, cornfields and mixed agriculture. Almost as old as the discipline of archaeology itself and given added weight by terms such as 'revolution' or 'watershed', this image has proved quite resistant to change. Yet it is so general that it has little contact with the evidence, and it seems to imply that food production dictates a specific set of attitudes and arrangements of people, labour and land. What it fails to capture is any intimate sense of the material world as it was lived and experienced by people.

So far as we can tell, much of Britain saw only limited woodland clearance at this time and there was a good deal of variation in the nature of cover within and between regions. Pine-dominated slopes in some areas; vast tracts of oak, elm and lime in others. There were dense, dark woodlands and more open forest. Within these conditions, many sites were established in clearings. Rather than a tradition of mixed agriculture with all that this entails, communities followed more diverse routines, their pattern sometimes varying from one region to another. For many, stock husbandry and limited cultivation made a significant contribution to the rhythm of daily and seasonal life. For others, the pattern of the year owed more to the character and availability of other species and, in many regions, hunting and collecting remained important.

This diversity resists simple generalisation and this is one reason why it is misleading to talk of a singular Neolithic subsistence 'package' as we sometimes do. What it was, and perhaps what different elements meant, could vary from one part of the country and from one time to another. This diversity also suggests that many communities followed routines which carried them around the landscape. Occupation could shift on a seasonal basis. It might also move every few years and at the timescale of generations. Certain locations saw only sporadic or episodic use, while others were marked by a more persistent human presence. River valleys and flood plains, varied uplands and coastlines, each was inhabited in different ways and at different times. Areas in which settlements might be established, animals pastured and crops grown, these zones also offered plants and animals for hunting and trapping. From a river valley settlement on the chalklands, people may have moved to where pasture, game or other resources could be found. For those near the sea or certain rivers, part of the year might revolve around the seasonal arrival of migratory fish. In parts of Cambridgeshire and Norfolk, stock rearing and horticulture on dry ground went hand in hand with the use of resources in the diverse environments of the Fens. Within these rhythms, the roll-call of specific places and times would have varied. Groups divided and combined in various ways at different seasons. More often than not, those groups comprised close kin.

These patterns of living and working can be glimpsed in stoneworking traditions. Although these vary from one setting to another, they often reveal a common emphasis on the working of cores to produce narrow flakes and

Figure 3 Earlier Neolithic hammerstone, blades, scrapers, fabricators and single piece sickles. (Photo: Museum of Archaeology and Anthropology, Cambridge.)

blades. Reflecting a consistency in the use of particular materials, many assemblages suggest the careful use of stone to produce portable and flexible tools. This may have been important at a time when residence and activity could move with the seasons; bags containing a hammer and stone for use may have hung from many shoulders. Dispersed across the landscape, these assemblages often appear to us as no more than surface scatters and chemical anomalies in the soil. Flakes, cores and tools brought to the surface by the plough, by development or by erosion, these scatters vary in their scale and composition. Where excavated, few produce features indicative of substantial structures and it is common to find sites defined by the presence of a few bowl-shaped pits. Many of these pits show signs of purposive filling, involving the careful deposition of pottery, tools, midden material and sometimes even fragments of people.

No doubt other sites remain to be discovered, in the bottom of river valleys or beneath peat or hillwash. Stake holes and other shallow settings have also been lost. However, many of these scatters sit uneasily within a model of mixed agriculture and stable residence. Some are small indeed. Identified through fieldwalking, they can be no more than twenty or thirty metres in diameter, comprising cores and waste, endscrapers and narrow flakes. An earlier Neolithic presence in particular places can even be marked by no more than one or two tools. Often these are the leaf-shaped arrowheads that appear at this time, lost in flight and in tangled undergrowth. Distributions such as these reflect the limited and sporadic use of particular locations; small camps established for part of a season, or places through which people passed, camps for herders or hunters, for those collecting clay or pausing near sacred ground.

Other scatters display different characteristics. Some take the form of more extensive spreads, their distribution being all that survives of one or two structures and middens that persisted for perhaps a generation. The range of artefacts in these settings can be more extensive. Cores and waste occur with burnt flint, scrapers, knives and other retouched pieces, a range that suggests a variety of tasks and a sense of duration. Sometimes the waste itself will indicate specific acts; the maintenance of flint and stone axes, the careful working of cores, the making of arrowheads, or the sharpening of scrapers. Undertaken on the margins of a settlement, near the fire of a hunting camp or as people sat watching the cattle, the ring of hammer on stone would have been heard at many times and places.

Other scatters are larger still. At places like Broome Heath in Norfolk or Tattershall Thorpe in Lincolnshire, excavation has revealed more extensive clusters of pits, stake holes and other features and a larger volume of stone. Similar evidence is scattered along the Thames gravels at places like Yarnton. These 'sites' are not always easy to interpret. Their scale may reflect the existence of settlements that comprised close kin and more distant relatives living side by side for several years. Alternatively, our evidence may reflect the passing of a different form of time. There were the hard grounds of winter,

Figure 4 Flaked and ground axes of flint and stone. (Photo: Museum of Archaeology and Anthropology, Cambridge.)

the pastures of late summer and the rich, light soils that had once been turned by dead kin. These were places to which people returned; each phase or generation of occupation adding to the sense of attachment that they held for an extended family. Sometimes there was even ground where kin and non-kin gathered for a short time, perhaps in step with the seasonal abundance of particular plants or animals. It is often difficult to choose between these readings, but the diversity of our evidence points to a richness and complexity in the practical topography of the landscape.

These observations erode at least part of the line that we often draw between the Mesolithic and the Neolithic. The communities that we call Neolithic used the landscape in similar ways to their forebears and this is also hinted at in the palaeoenvironmental record. Behind the appearance of cereal pollen, itself varied from region to region, our evidence suggests that sporadic clearance and woodland management did not spring up with the first crop of corn nor with the birth of the first calf. These practices are just as visible in the later Mesolithic. People had initiated and responded to change in these diverse ecologies for many generations.

There are also continuities in stoneworking. Like the first pottery or monuments, we recognise the onset of the Neolithic through the appearance of new tools: ground axes of flint and stone and the leaf-shaped arrowheads

mentioned above. These innovations are important, but there are also traditions that went relatively unchanged. Customary practices of stone procurement can persist across the line that we have drawn; the same places and the
same patterns of selection. Similar attitudes to core reduction can also be
traced in both periods. Often extensively worked, cores show a concern with
the production of regular flakes and blades, with the careful maintenance of
platforms and the application of subtle technical skills. It is not uncommon to
find a mixture of material reflecting the use of a location in both periods.
This was not always the case. Many scatters can be attributed to one period or
the other and there are gaps in our distributions. It is clear that the later fifth
and early fourth millennia saw the opening up of new ground. Communities
settling in a river valley or on the margins of uplands might do so in places
with no strong history of residence or clearance. But often the traces of the
past were there to be seen. Palimpsests remind us that despite many changes,
people in the earlier Neolithic inhabited the land in ways that sometimes had
a long ancestry indeed. Seasonal routines of movement by small, dispersed
communities involved passage along well-worn pathways and a return to
places that had been used in earlier years or by older generations.

    Continuities in the pattern and tempo of life also suggest a constancy in
ways of thinking about people, the land and the past. Communities whose
lives involve a degree of routine movement don't always perceive the landscape as an object to be parcelled up or divided into discrete entities. Instead,
they often emphasise concepts of place and pathway which may overlap or cut
across one another. The ties that bind people to these places often involve the
evocation of a sense of tenure to be renewed rather than territory to be held.
This tenure is often grounded in a sense of ancestry, sustained through origin
myths and identified with the physical evidence of the past encountered in

Figure 5 Earlier Neolithic pottery (drawing: Chris Jones).

the course of practical experience. Social boundaries of various forms can be recognised and respected, at times they can be actively contested. But their horizons can retain a fluidity as communities combine, divide and relocate in tempo with seasonal cycles and as one generation gives way to another.

Like the stories that they told around their fires, much of the significance that people worked into the land remains beyond our grasp. Some have argued that the Neolithic world was structured around a symbolic opposition between the domestic and the wild, seeing this as a frame upon which other divisions of identity and authority could be mapped – old and young; kin and non-kin; male and female. These ideas have their attractions and it is likely that the customary use of domesticated plants and animals did bring with it new concerns and attitudes. However, rigid divisions between culture and nature, between the tame and the wild, do little justice to the meanings that people wove into the land, plants and animals around them. In all societies, the classification of the world often owes much to specific and contingent concepts of history, identity and the supernatural. We are no exception to this rule. The practical or medicinal potentials of different materials may be recognised, but their significance is often understood through reference to other themes. Ancestral powers and histories are sometimes vested in trees or stones, and spirits of the dead may be seen in their forms. Qualities of permanence and decay, of strength or pollution can be ascribed to different materials and implicated in the manner of their use. Even rivers or ridge tops can occupy positions in myth, these qualities being drawn upon where those features serve as boundaries or places for spiritual communication.

Prominent features in origin stories, and often shrouded with proscription and taboo, materials and places are drawn upon as people renew their connections with the land and as they cross important thresholds in their lives. Rites of passage often involve separation from the community at large and visits to sacred sites can be pivotal moments in the transition from one state of being to another. Ritualised consumption can be used to occasion movement between worlds or to mark the acquisition of a new position within the community. Like the right to participate in these events, knowledge of certain places might be acquired as one moved from adolescence to adulthood or from one kin group to another on marriage. Some stories may have only been heard by the elders or by ritual specialists; the telling and hearing of others may have been the prerogative either of women or of men.

What was it like to occupy these conditions? What did it mean to live and labour in woodland settings or to move in step with herds? There may be much that we cannot know, but we can recognise at least some of the ways in which routine life contributed to the playing out of relations between dispersed communities. One of the curious features in many depictions of the Neolithic is the position of woodlands. Stands of trees are a common element, but they often appear in deep perspective, a static backdrop to events and archetypes. This is not altogether surprising. We often assume that the onset of food production necessarily went hand in hand with wholesale

Figure 6 Coppiced woodland.

clearance and this may be part of the reason why trees are so often consigned to the background. Where mentioned at all, they tend to be the victims of an inexorable and inevitable process of deforestation. This caricature does little justice to our evidence. In reality, woodlands were a commonplace in many areas. From extensive mixed deciduous tracts to birch, scrub and dense fen margins, they were both the setting and the medium for much of life. Even areas that we might now call wildwood were forests with long histories of use and reuse. Places for food, for living and perhaps even places of spiritual danger, forests carried the marks of a human and ancestral presence. They were the familiar frame in which many people's lives unfolded.

Communities had moved in and out of step with the rhythms of woodlands long before the Neolithic. The manipulation of forest cover had been a regular feature in the lives of gatherers and hunters and this remained the norm for later generations. Cut close to the earth or relieved of their boughs, many trees generate new shoots and an abundance of leaves that are easily reached and often favoured by browsing animals. Where practised, the firing of woodland or scrub encourages similar patterns of regeneration. Alterations on the margins or in the interior of forests had long been used to influence the movement of deer. Sometimes this involved the use of natural clearings – places where lightning had struck, where trees were thrown by the wind or stripped of their bark by browsing. In the dense, tangled forests of the time, these natural clearings may have been of great importance. At other times, fire, ring barking and the axe played their part in more purposive episodes of clearance. Renewed over time, these clearings were places to which both animals and people would return, where prey might be found, and old camps could be re-established in certain seasons. Scattered along traditional routes, they could be places of chance acquaintance – where members of one kin group might meet others, where stories might be told, news passed and materials traded.

Clearance, of course, serves other purposes. The removal of woodland cover and the maintenance of grassland is an important element in the management of domesticated animals, whether in an infield or in more distant, seasonal, pastures. It is also a common precursor to settlement, the clearing of ground being one of the ways in which people may make a commitment to place. In a country where unchecked woodland regeneration can have a significant impact in a handful of years, that commitment would need to be made and made again. We should not underestimate the importance that routine clearance may have held in both mundane and monumental settings.

With woodland management comes the creation of resources. Valuable tools and hafts can be cultivated over a handful of years and structural timbers harvested from one generation to the next. Coppicing and shredding generate fodder for animals. They also foster the growth of underwood for tool hafts or the flexible rods that can be woven into the fabric of buildings, baskets and hurdles. Evidence from the diverse 'wetlands' that still survive demonstrates the knowledge that people had of these potentials. In areas like the Fens or the Somerset Levels, waterlogging and the rapid accumulation of peat preserved timbers which hint at sophisticated traditions of management and use. Trackways across the Levels reflect an investment of time and knowledge in the cutting, cultivation and working of timber, and in the creation of paths between places. Features like the Sweet Track in Somerset, which linked two areas of drier ground, provide a good case in point. The evidence of tree rings suggests an unusually precise date of around 3806 BC for the construction of this trackway and at least ten wood species are represented. Ash, hazel and oak predominate and it is likely that these resources were drawn from more than one woodland stand. The inventory from the site is impressive: some 6,000 pegs, 400 metres of planking and 2,000 metres of rails. There are freshly cut poles, fast grown and likely to be the result of careful and consistent coppicing, and there are older, seasoned timbers, oak planking and rails made from wood cut a generation before. Oliver Rackham has pointed out that in the conditions of the time, trees like birch and alder would have been abundant and close at hand. They would have been available while the track was being built and maintained, yet they were passed over in favour of resources brought in from elsewhere. These patterns of selection imply traditions of working woodland that stretched across the landscape and even across generations.

Modified, extended and maintained over time, features such as the Sweet Track linked the clearings and camps of certain seasons or the dwellings of different families. The materials required for their construction necessitated planning, agreement and a sense of temporality that went beyond the short term and the immediate. Sometimes good for stock to eat and often good to work with, these different materials grew at different rhythms. Coppice stools and pollards are often cut in the winter after the sap has fallen. In upland areas, shredded trees could produce leafy hay for use in harsh winters and these needed tending every few years. Tasks such as these may have been tied into the seasonal round and into longer-term cycles of movement and residence. Ring barking itself demanded an acknowledgement of these longer cycles, a form of clearance that might stretch over ten or fifteen years.

This variety was important for the significance that people attached to particular places. Important as a repository from which resources could be drawn, woodlands were also sources of metaphor, mnemonic and symbol. On a day-to-day basis and in the course of the annual cycle, the condition of forests provided evidence of activities conducted in the recent past. A small group moving on a hunting trip would have recognised the subtle changes in the state of the ground that spoke of human action and the relative timescales involved. Returning to a clearing meant an encounter with the past and perhaps with others. How far had new growth encroached on the summer camp of the previous year? Had others been this way? How long had they stayed and what had they done? In a landscape composed of small, dispersed communities, these readings provided an important source of information

Figure 7 The Sweet Track, Somerset Levels. (Photo courtesy of the Somerset Levels Project.)

and a sense of the histories behind the routines that people followed. With the clearance of low cover would come the discovery of the old hearths, middens and scatters of broken stone that also spoke of the past, and of a human presence. Even clearings and changes in the forest brought about by fire, disease or rapid erosion might have been seen as much through the imagination as through the practical eye. Perhaps the ground opened up by lightning or the wind reflected the help of the ancestors in guiding settlement among the living.

The redolences of woodlands could be acknowledged over longer time-scales. With the passing of generations, the state of forests was a testament to the character and depth of the roots that linked people to the land. Surface scatters containing both later Mesolithic and earlier Neolithic stone tools suggest that those roots may have sometimes extended far into the past. Where settlements were moved or re-established over these longer timescales, abandoned sites could be distinguished from their surrounds and the presence of large, straight timber may have been as evocative as it was practicable. Returning to regenerated clearings and gardens involved the felling of timbers once set as coppice by grandparents or by distant cousins. Located in oral tradition, the places where long-dead kin once lived and worked could be recognised and remembered; new settlements were grafted onto the roots of the old. Long forgotten but still acknowledged were other places where people traced the actions of spirits. Landmarks in the geography of myth, these were the traces of an ancestral hunting camp or a garden where the first crops had been grown. Nearby was the river on which people had first travelled here, their bones being returned to its currents on death. Clearing the margins of old camps and gardens, felling trees, or cutting back new growth around a tomb, tending and reworking the land offered quiet confirmation of the histories and genealogies that bound people to particular places.

Beyond the margins of woodlands and linked by well-worn paths and rivers lay pastures and cultivated ground; features in the pollen record from many regions. Interpretation of this evidence is not without its problems: pollen from different species occurs in varying quantities and it can travel over different distances. Some species, like lime, may be under-represented and it is not always easy to specify the extent of grassland or cultivation, nor the lengths of time over which these patches endured. What these patterns do confirm is the importance of livestock. Sheep would have been a common sight on open ground in many areas, and pigs may have foraged on the margins of settlements and beneath the woodland canopy. These animals were of practical and social significance. Pigs that broke and turned the earth with their snouts could become an important gift at a feast. Wool might be traded or turned into a garment that was handed down, like the skills required in weaving, from one generation to another. Whether either was regarded as a source of value or as an active symbol is unclear, but both offered a contrast to animals drawn from the wild and a different relation to people. They could be accumulated and owned in different ways. Their genealogies could be known and influenced so that blood lines were also ties between kin and histories of relations.

One species dominates our attention. One of the most common domesticates recognised during excavations, cattle appear to have been of particular importance for many communities. How did these animals operate in the lives and experiences of people? Even a partial reliance on cattle creates a series of practical requirements for small communities and these are often meshed into other concerns. For much of Britain, it is perhaps inappropriate to think in terms of full-blown pastoralism, or of large nomadic communities negotiating equally large herds across regions. Rather more common was a pattern which saw communities moving relatively small herds between vale and wold. The distances involved may often have been no more than a handful of days. But the seasonal round may have been just that; a cycle that took people into different areas and into different combinations at particular times of the year. In the Peak District, the annual cycle saw people moving between valleys and higher clearings on the limestone and the gritstones of the Dark Peak and East Moors. In areas such as southern Dorset, cycles of movement carried groups from coast to chalk upland. In these, as in other regions, many places had a season.

Stock husbandry also involved changes in the scale and composition of herds across the seasons. Individual animals may have moved between communities for a variety of reasons, and different herds were probably brought together at certain times. Sometimes these changes went in step with practical necessity: disease and in-breeding can create major problems for small pools of stock. Late summer may have seen the bull of one family serve the cows of another, with calves being born as the earth itself was renewed in the spring. Often however, the conditions which prompted the movement of animals had as much, if not more, to do with the working of relationships between people.

Apart from their significance in providing meat and milk and as a source of leather or bone, cattle provided an important structure in the lives of Neolithic communities. At one level, the animals themselves may have provided metaphors for the constitution of groups and the identities of particular people. Patterns and thresholds in the lives of cattle may have been drawn upon to evoke similar themes in their lives; gestation, maturity, renewal; castration, strength and fertility. The changing scale of herds would have sometimes been in step with the coming together of people from different communities and this too may have held a metaphoric significance for the ties that stretched between those groups. This may be part of the reason why beef was eaten and cattle bones were deposited with some formality at a number of enclosures.

Cattle may have also been an important source of wealth and standing. The capacity to hold and exchange cattle was probably a prerogative of particular age grades, and animals may have moved between kin groups as marriage gifts, or in settlement of blood feuds. On and off the hoof, cattle may have passed between trading partners, their passage creating relations that went beyond the horizons of immediate kinship. The success with which families were able to sustain herds in the face of problems may have been taken as an index of their standing in relation to the supernatural. From drought and disease through to raids and rustling, livestock, like crops, were vulnerable. Their health and fertility could be guarded by appeals to the ancestors and these concerns may have been addressed in the feasts and offerings given at tombs and in other settings. These were entities with the power to influence fortune among the living. They could curse as well as bless and their continued support required respect and observance. Under these circumstances, the renown of a particular group or family head may have been enhanced where these appeals appeared to fall on sympathetic ears. This may be part of the reason why cattle are found in a number of tombs. 'Head and hoof' burials have been recorded at a number of sites and at tombs like the Beckhampton barrow near Avebury, the bodies of cattle were sometimes treated as if they were human bodies. These animals could be drawn upon to stand for particular categories or qualities of people. Taken from the herd of close kin, a slaughtered cow signified the ties that bound the living to a passing generation. Given as a gift to the dead and eaten at a funeral, the animal established relations between the mourners. Treated like the human body, the carcass signalled a close identification of people through their herds.

The seasonal round that grew out of the keeping of livestock provided rhythms that animated the movement and interaction of varied numbers of people. It was a frame around which other activities and events could be ordered. Communities may have travelled to periodic gatherings with their herds, or moved in step with their hooves as one season gave way to another. Winter drew the cattle in while summer separated the herd, and perhaps particular people, from the broader group. These cycles made sense in what we regard as practical terms. But they also provided a medium through which communities made sense of other aspects of their lives. They created a routine context in which encounters with neighbours, distant kin or relative strangers could be anticipated and undertaken. Where separation from the broader community was linked to concepts of liminality, seasonal movements with cattle may have been linked into rites of passage. Perhaps there were times when elders took children off to late summer pastures, explaining the practical and ancestral landmarks they encountered on the way.

Behind the animals themselves lay the grasslands, paths and woodland fodder that were crucial to their survival. In the patchwork landscape of the earlier Neolithic, woods and areas of cultivation placed constraints upon movement, and the apportioning of grazing land required negotiation, consensus and even conflict between communities. Had someone else's animals eaten vital crops? Had stock been rustled or lost in a failed marriage? Were another group encroaching on pastures or clearings that had long been used by generations of a certain lineage? Had a herd been cursed or polluted? The persistence of grassland in the pollen record attests to the maintenance of these resources and it is likely that land used periodically might have sometimes been an object of competition. Clearance itself may have been implicated in this process. The patchwork was far from static, and the removal of woodland would have sometimes cut across the pathways that linked winter with summer and one community with another.

These observations return us to the pits that often lie beneath scatters of broken stone. The contents of these features often display an order which is difficult to explain as the random or gradual accumulation of rubbish, however we choose to define the term. Pottery sherds may show considered selection and placement, and material from middens or episodes of consumption is not uncommon. In cases like the pit near the River Snail mentioned at the beginning of this chapter, it is sometimes the residues of particular forms of working that are emphasised. The common context of these features suggests that the gathering and burial of material in this way was often a localised act. Undertaken on settlements and limited camps, the practice of breaking the earth and planting cultural remains was an event attended by a relatively small company. The full significance of this practice remains beyond our grasp, but it may be that these acts were a medium through which communities renewed their sense of tenure with particular places. They held evidence for past relations and events. This may have been of great importance where seasonal and even generational cycles carried people from one setting to another.

For those who were present, the gathering together and burial of material drew attention to the practical ties that bound communities to specific locales. Some contained the detritus of daily life: food remains, and tools that had associations with specific people or tasks. There was the red-brown pottery that had been made by familiar hands, a vessel that was used to prepare and present food and to carry offerings. In its form could be traced the local knowledge of clays and tempers that was handed down from one generation to the next. There were other sherds that had once contained gifts, their presence a reminder of events and relations with others. Perhaps there were times when the breaking of a vessel, like the smashing or burial of a tool, brought a relationship or even a person to a close. Where included, fragments of the dead, like the tools people used in life, brought specific genealogies into focus. Some pits brought together the remains of a feast: a marriage, a death, an important bout of trading or a meeting between family heads. Created as people left for a season, the filling of pits, like the planting of crops, offered the hope of renewal, regeneration and return. Filled at the conclusion of a local ceremony, a pit tied an event and the relations it involved to the land itself. Here was the place where people had met, where bonds had been forged and tensions resolved. Here lay the tools that had been used by a mother or a son before their death in early winter. For those who returned and remembered, these features provided reminders of the past that lay behind an old clearing or camp.

How did people think about themselves? What ideas were implicated in activities such as the cutting and filling of pits on settlements? We have talked of extended families, but these were far from isolated. Dispersed and fragmented though the land may have been, networks of communication stretched back and forth between people born to different lines of descent. Although we cannot be certain, people probably understood themselves in relation to concepts of lineage or even clan membership. These social geographies were far from static. Extended families were caught up in shifting webs of kin ties, alliances and affiliations. Many of the threads in these webs were mediated by various forms of exchange. Marriage involved the movement of people as well as goods or gifts between communities. It also brought with it new rights of access and obligations to participate in both practical and ceremonial activity. Whether these relations involved matrilocal or patrilocal patterns of residence cannot be determined. Both may have been recognised, but these ties might not persist and failed marriages could create friction between groups.

Marriage was just one of the ways in which relations between communities could be worked. Obligations incurred through feasting or exchange might lead some to wield a local authority over others, just as the elders might purport to stand above their juniors. These claims were contested and reworked as a regular feature in the playing out of relations between communities. Tensions could even manifest themselves in outright conflict; rustling, blood feuds, and more overtly ceremonial forms of fighting. Convention and taboo probably surrounded the question of who could fight, and even where and when such events could be staged. No doubt there were many times when people voted with their feet. Yet in different regions and at different times, endemic, graded warfare may have been a commonplace. This idea finds vivid expression where bodies have been penetrated by arrows, the stone tip retaining an association in death. More often than not, these associations are with adult men. There were times when argument and negotiation revolved around questions of access; to hunting grounds or grazing, to old settlement areas, or perhaps to sources of stone. At others, questions of standing and renown were brought into sharp relief. Yet often it was the ancestors and their powers that were the focus of attention. Proximity and the right to speak on their behalf could be a privilege of position and an expression of authority. It could also be drawn upon to serve particular interests.

Woven into this tapestry were more basic threads; the taken-for-granteds of self, community and the world that cut across the lines of kinship. These attitudes may have been recognised as much in the breach as in the observance and were highlighted in different ways according to company and context. Distinctions may have been drawn between children and adults and between elders and their juniors. Gender categories were also recognised and, like age grades, these would have changed over the course of a lifetime. Amongst other things, initiatory rites of passage probably involved inclusion in gender groupings that were a common frame for much of life. Certain activities and events would have brought women together, others would have involved only men. Perhaps men were linked to the herding of stock while women identified more closely with activities such as cultivation. Here again, much remains uncertain, but through these times came the recognition of identity and the renewal of kinship, the settling of disputes and, inevitably, the talk which passed between people. Who was sick? Who had died? Who had been seen and what did they trade? Who had broken with custom or convention? These events, in their turn, were grounded in origin myths and concepts of ancestral time which were shared by many. Stories may have been told of the creation of the land and its first occupation, of mythic events and ancestral struggles. These stories may have had a timeless quality, perhaps like the ancestral realm itself, but they could be linked to the present by specific ancestors and long genealogies. Acknowledged in the pattern of daily life, these values and distinctions were brought into focus through rites of passage, oral tradition and the passing on of practical and ritual knowledge. They could also be reworked by shifts in the fortunes of a family and in broader regimes of kinship and affiliation.

4 Keeping to the path

The summer had been long. The land had been dry for months, hard to imagine it had ever been otherwise. Old pastures had turned yellow and thin. Scrub had been like tinder waiting for a spark. When the new ground was fired for the following year, the air grew heavy with ash. Those skilled in the setting and tending of the flames had been smeared with charcoal for days.

Now things were changing. Clouds had swollen and gathered beyond the hills and all could smell the rain they carried. The winds had found their breath once more, and it would not be long before the trees began to yield to the slow death of winter. There was much to be done. The herd would soon return and there were crops to be gathered before they drew close. The corn and the nuts were almost ripe. Sedge had been cut and stacked to replenish thatch, and the rafters of the houses were stocked with dried meat. More would be needed, but first there was the track.

The two families had been talking of the task for some time. The elders agreed that the path between their lodges would not last another winter. Without work, it would be lost, drawn down by the spirits in the marsh. They would cut new poles from the old stand near the spring and work together in the splitting of fresh planks. It would take three of the oaks that had fallen in the last storms.

Two of the younger men had left the day before. They had gone upriver to hunt, climbing east to where the forest met the open country. There was a flurry of argument at their leaving. The older men and women said they should hunt another time, that they should stay and help in the cutting of the timbers and the hammering of poles. The distance was unnecessary. There was plenty of game to be had close at hand if you knew how to wait. Voices had been raised and there was talk of respect, the elders trying to shame the young. It did not matter, they said. There would be plenty still to do when they returned. Besides, what use was a path when there was not enough meat in the lodge to keep them through the winter? They left soon after, taking the longer trail in the hope that they would meet with cousins and a chance to trade.

The stand was only a short walk from the clearing, reached in the time it took to draw milk from the herd. Dense and varied, much of it had not been cut for years.

On the margins, the rods were no thicker than a child's arm, their circumference a measure of the four summers that had passed since a few stools were cut for hafts. Further in, the poles grew wider and taller. They were already standing when the lodges were built, a legacy from kin who had lived on this ground two generations before. As they cleared back the scrub and set to the task, there was talk of earlier times and of the souls who lingered near the spring. A few kept one eye on the shadows as they went.

There was a pattern to the work. Some bent to cut the poles where they sprang from the stools. Using short, angled strokes, they cut into the wood on three sides, creating much of the point before the poles came away. That was how it was always done; you could still see the scars from before. Others set to trimming, sharpening the points and stripping thin shoots from the sides of each shaft. The poles would be carried back to the marsh at their full length. It was easier that way. Once there, they would be cut into stakes before being set in place.

A few worked away from the stand; close by but invisible in the tangle. They had started splitting the oaks two days before and already there were seven good planks. Stood in a line along what remained of the trunk, they discussed where best to place their wedges. As always, there was more than one opinion to be heard before a consensus was reached. You had to know when to push and when to pause; the tree had to let go of the plank. If you pushed too hard, the wood would tear. At least the timber was still soft enough to work. Once fallen oaks had seasoned, they were harder than stone.

Caught up in the task, one of the older men struggled to free a pole that would not leave the stand. He had been working for some time and his arm was tired and heavy. His axe turned slightly in his hand. At the next blow, the axe bounced off the wood and, as it did, a flake came away from the edge. Reaching down, he picked it up and with a muttered curse, placed it back against the facet it had left. A perfect fit. There would be a day of grinding before the axe was keen again, another before it was back in its haft. Putting the tool to one side, he used his weight to pull the pole away. It bent and creaked before finally splitting from the base. It was not a clean break and he cursed again. A tongue of bark and wet sapwood protruded from the end. The old man pulled and the tongue came away, leaving a white groove down the side of the pole over a hands' span long. It was no matter. The scar would be lost once the point was cut.

Up on open ground, the two hunters looked back at the smoke which spiralled from their lodge. Camped near the circle where the old ones gathered, they ate strips from the stag caught just after dawn. A day's walk now separated them, but they had yet to catch any sign of their cousins. There had been a solitary hearth along the way, but it was cold, the ashes scattered long before their arrival. Soon they would have to return, following the path and their obligation to help with the track. The stag would make them welcome, but they had missed the chance to trade. More than that, they had missed the chance of news. So long as hunger remained a half-remembered ache, a fresh story was worth more than meat. They would talk instead of the state of the ground; of the way they had walked silently, and how the stag had offered himself to them.

Work began at the edge of the marsh. Despite the long months of heat, the wet ground still sucked at the ankles. Poles and planks from the stand had started to arrive and these were quickly cut to size. Some worked thin withies into hurdles for the track. Others helped in the cutting of joints for the frame. There was talk of how new timbers were to be added; sniggering when the old man spoke of his broken axe. That wasn't news.

A few began to manoeuvre the first stakes into position, probing to find the best angle and the strongest purchase. Ignoring instructions shouted from drier ground, they felt for older wood that lay beneath the surface. It would be two days before the planks were laid, several more before the task was complete. It had to be done right. The frame had to be strong or the way would not last, and bad work showed disrespect to those who had kept the path before. Sharp joints and other offerings would persuade the dead to carry the timbers on their backs. With their help, it would not be swallowed by the marsh.

Before long, the stakes were being pushed and hammered into place. Greenwood poles slid down, taking their lead from blackened stumps that had stood for years. Driven home, the fresh points cut through older timbers that had softened in the wet. The old track received them, made them part of itself. Planks set in place a generation before pressed down on others long forgotten. Seen from below, the task had no end, only pauses.

Figure 8

5 Working stone

Up on the chalk of the Sussex Downs are earthworks which mark an earlier Neolithic presence. At Blackpatch, Cissbury and Harrow Hill, hollows, scoops and banks give the land a pock-marked appearance. Excavations have shown that these places once offered a dramatic contrast of colour and form to their wooded surrounds. Hidden beneath the turf are the shafts, galleries and knapping floors of flint mines. This had once been land to which people had come to hunt and to collect resources offered by the forest. Perhaps they had also come to collect the dark flint that lay close to the surface, where nodules sometimes took the shape of animals or people. But early in the fourth millennium, that process of winning stone from the earth took on different characteristics. In the south and east, people began to cut deep to where the floorstone lay – the good stone, dark and consistent. In the north and west, they traced sources upstream; working stone on mountains and escarpments. Features now in landscapes of leisure; places for picnics and for walking, these sources no longer echo to the crack of stone. Yet in these features we can follow traditions of working that were once a regular feature in people's lives. Surface scatters can tell us much, but we can take the picture further by exploring these traditions.

This was a time when people's understandings of the land hung upon places and pathways, upon concepts of seasonal tenure and ancestry. The shifting mosaic of grass, woodland, scrub and cultivated earth grew out of the actions and the histories of people. It lent an order to their experience and understanding of the world around them. Vital for subsistence, this mosaic was also a medium through which people marked and read the land in terms of its cultural and historical significance. For the most part, we can do no more than guess at the content of stories or the significance that the land held for different people. We can assume though, that their telling was often bound up in the mastery of material traditions. Acquiring the skills required in the mixing and firing of clays, in moving herds, working stone or building houses also meant acknowledging other themes and values. Where were different clays or pastures to be found? When were they best collected or used? Who could undertake these tasks and who could not? No doubt many tasks were undertaken by all, some even involving contact and co-operation between different kin groups. Others were the preserve of only certain people – women rather than men; close kin rather than strangers; adults rather than children. Like the sharing of food, activities brought different people together and stressed different aspects of their identities at certain places and times. Visits to particular settings also meant approaching sites of ancestral importance and this lent a gravity and, perhaps, a timeless quality to the tasks that were performed and the relations they involved. The creation of cultivation plots or houses, the management of stock, the maintenance of grazing rights or the hunting of game; all were practices in which different relations and identities could be brought into focus. They were also contexts in which tensions might arise and in which some might come to hold authority and influence over others.

We can catch some of the ways in which practical and social were bound together in the working of stone. Different raw materials and even different pieces of the same stone can offer unique potentials and problems. Yet we often find an order in the procurement and production of tools, and in this order we can explore how material tradition bound people to place and to each other. Just as it had always been, the conditions under which people acquired stone in the earlier Neolithic were far from uniform. Material might be acquired by chance, from a river bank or from a tree throw. It could also be won through the use of local sources, through various forms of transaction, or by visits to more distant places. Sometimes sustained over centuries, these varied traditions had important consequences for the ways in which people came to understand themselves and their relationships with others. Like techniques of working, some of these traditions stretched back into the Mesolithic; others marked a break with the past. Materials that had been worked for many generations continued to be used and the histories and genealogies attached to their sources cut across the boundary that we place between the two periods. Other sources rise to archaeological prominence with the onset of the Neolithic and this may indicate important changes in the significance that was sometimes attached to stone procurement and tool production.

Complements rather than alternatives, these varied traditions of procurement had redolences that could be appreciated in a range of ways. Growing up in a particular community involved learning the seasonal pattern of the land and its history. As an aspect of this knowledge, and no doubt cut through with myth, were themes related to the winning and working of stone. Where were long-used sources? Where might one find chance exposures? When was it appropriate to travel to collect stone? In maintaining these traditions among kin, communities maintained their attachment to the landscape itself and passed that connection down across generations. Returning to local gravel terraces or outcrops, to beaches or pockets of chert or clay-with-flints, the young would learn how to select, test and work stone. Moving along a river valley, they might learn how to read pebbles as signs of a source upstream. Observation and instruction probably went hand in hand with the telling of stories about the past, and all around would be evidence of earlier visits and similar tasks. Who had created these pockets and seams and who had found them? Who could work there and who could not? Who needed to be consulted?

Sometimes tied to herding or the hunting of game, these tasks made the landscape familiar. Learning to look and learning to work also meant learning about one's place in the community. At Ramsey in the Cambridgeshire Fens, a small cap of sand and gravel rises above an area of more marshy ground still covered with peat. On this low, dry hill, a dense scatter of flint is all that remains of a place where small groups came, bringing with them the nodules of flint they had won from gravel beds and river banks in the area. Despite a lot of waste material, there are few tools in this assemblage, and no features beneath the surface. However, there are a number of retouched flakes and some burnt flint, a material which speaks of hearths and other activities. These are the characteristics of a place that was visited perhaps on a periodic basis and one that saw a limited range of stoneworking tasks.

A closer inspection of this scatter is revealing. Many blades and narrow flakes occur on the hill, but they are more than outweighed by the cores from which they were struck. These cores bear the scars of consistent and almost obsessive knapping, with regular working extended until they were exhausted, or reduced to heavily fractured fragments. Other characteristics can also be seen. Exhausted though they are, some of the cores have clearly been worked with a high degree of precision, control and anticipation. Careful trimming, shifting of angles and the maintenance of working faces are all evidenced in these pieces. These were the by-products of accustomed hands, for whom working had become as much a rhythm as a set of procedures. Side by side with these cores we find others with a rather different signature. Once again, the production of blades and narrow flakes seems to have been a recognised goal, but here it is more difficult to see the same concern with control and anticipation. Errors and miss-hits are more common and this suggests a certain awkwardness and lack of familiarity: the principles were understood but the practice was not quite there.

We can understand these patterns in a number of ways, but two themes are important here. The balance of cores to blades and narrow flakes suggests that many products from these moments of working were removed from this place. They were taken off to be used elsewhere, and thus they drop out of archaeological view. Perhaps their uses lay in the Fens, at other camps or places where certain tasks would be performed. Perhaps they were for the return to the community, after time spent away with the cattle or for other reasons. These questions carry us beyond the margins of this cap of sand and gravel. The signatures of working revealed in the cores also suggest differences of skill or concern. They might reflect the activities of people who visited this place at different times. Another possibility is that they revolve around divisions of age and experience. Perhaps some worked while others struggled to learn, and out of that relationship sprang a local sense of position and seniority.

Routine traditions of procurement and stoneworking probably sustained quite localised concepts of identity, but it is often difficult to say much about their content. On settlements, it is likely that the creation of middens and working areas on the margins or among buildings added resolution to the spatial order of daily experience. From these arrangements may have come the recognition of close kinship, personal identity and position within the community. Sometimes these themes may have been hung on the production and use of specific tools. Leaf-shaped arrowheads, laurel leaves and sickles suggest a concern with hunting, harvesting and perhaps fighting, however graded or ritualised the latter may have been. They also betray an increased concern with the execution of careful patterns of bifacial working, pressure flaking and invasive retouch that went beyond the satisfaction of material need. The same might be said for axes and adzes. Practicable though they undoubtedly were, the making and using of these tools helped to sustain ideas about individual roles and responsibilities.

Without more detailed evidence, there is much that remains unclear, but we can assume that beyond more persistent settlements and in seasonal settings, spreads of tools, waste and burnt stone confirmed that cycles of movement and action were grounded in history. The encounter with stone-working debris in an overgrown clearing helped to define the connotations of that place and may even have influenced where people worked on their return. Discarded cores and waste flakes may have signalled the activities undertaken in the past, or they may have simply been recognised as rock that had been transformed by earlier generations. Here was a place where the earth had been broken, where nodules found beneath the surface were tested by tapping and the removal of one or two flakes. Here was a larger spread of tools and waste, and of burnt stone scattered between old coppice stands. Who had spent time here and what did this scatter – like the coppice – say about the nature and duration of their stay? Where different raw materials and even ways of working were associated with specific groups, these too may have contributed to people's perceptions of the past and present of specific locations. Perhaps the roots of these scatters sometimes stretched beyond the genealogies of specific communities and into the ancestral past itself.

Played out across the landscape, the procurement and working of stone could be meshed into other concerns. Differences in raw materials from one area to another created a potential for various forms of exchange and this had important consequences for relations between groups. The circulation of material could be a political act, caught up in marriages, blood fines and prestation, but it was also a medium through which ties between people were maintained through barter and other forms of trading partnership. Kin in a nearby valley might be a routine source of quartered nodules; others met on seasonal trails gave access to different stones and tools.

Often these different material conditions were eroded by periodic move-ment, a pattern we can trace in southern Dorset. Here communities followed an annual cycle that wound between the lowlands and the rolling chalk that we now call Cranborne Chase, an area long renowned for its high density of long barrows. Separating these two zones, and running for some eleven kilometres lies the Dorset Cursus, a massive monument of parallel banks which dips and rises across undulations in the chalk. People may have often passed this monument in the company of cattle and a few kin, but there were times when it provided a focus and a frame for more signal events. Embellished and extended over time, perhaps over generations, and aligned on long barrows and the midwinter sunset, many have seen this monument as a place of gatherings and processions, of ancestral worship and rites which linked the living to the dead and to the heavens. Access to the interior and to the secrets of this monument may have been restricted at certain times, and the right to move along its course may have defined people in terms of their authority.

The details of this monument have dominated our attention, but here we can focus on an aspect of the landscape setting of both the cursus and the clusters of barrows. These sites mimic the general distribution of areas of clay-with-flints, sources from which communities gained workable stone. Some, such as Thickthorn Down long barrow, were even built over the mouths of old quarry pits. This had long been an area to which people from different communities came to collect and work stone. Visited on a periodic, perhaps seasonal, basis this was a time and a place where people from different groups might expect to meet; where transactions were undertaken, information passed and relations renewed. With time, this pattern of procurement became embedded in animal husbandry as well as hunting and collecting, the creation of areas of grazing bringing with it changes in the land and new concerns. It may have been the need to renew a sense of tenure with these places that was addressed through the creation and repeated use of ancestral houses, and it was through the reworking of these earlier Neolithic conditions that the cursus arose. Communally constructed and a focus for ancestral and other rites, the cursus created a more proscribed arena in which people from different groups came together.

While they differ in many respects from the patterns seen in Dorset, other places rich in raw materials may have witnessed periodic encounters between people from different communities. Along parts of the Yorkshire coast, the red-brown cliffs of glacial till contain flint that occurs in a variety of forms, colours and qualities. Winter storms would bring fresh nodules to light and, in certain seasons, smoke from the fires of a number of camps may have risen above the coast. On the high chalklands too, large nodules of flint could be recovered, often distinctive and sometimes suitable for making larger tools. Along the Trent valley workable nodules could be found in the gravels, while in the Peak District seams of dense, black chert could be found in the sides of steep limestone valleys. Visited by many generations of gatherers and hunters, these sources continued to be used by the herders who lived across the limestone and the grits. The collection, testing and working of stone at these places brought people into routine contact with others. Out of that contact came the renewal of ties of affiliation that stretched between groups. On occasion, friction may have arisen from the breaking of traditional rights of access to sources of workable and perhaps even spiritually important stone.

Sometimes it seems that people were even more exacting in their definition of appropriate times and places for procurement and production. Mines and quarries emerged during the course of the earlier Neolithic, locales in which a particular emphasis was placed upon the production of axes of flint and stone. These tools were also made at other times and in other settings, but the dominance of rejects and distinctive flakes at many mines and quarries suggests a close connection between place and artefact. Eminently practicable, axes and adzes were often ground and polished and, beyond their functions, they appear to have served as tokens of identity – their possession and use marking distinctions of age and gender. Many accounts talk of a symbolic and practical link with men and, while axes were probably used by women too, there may have been times when these more categoric links were brought into focus. Axes and adzes also moved from hand to hand and from one generation to another as goods and as gifts. Passing along the lines of obligation and affiliation that stretched between different groups, the circulation of axes may have been an important medium through which a variety of social relations were reproduced. Played out across many generations, these traditions of circulation carried axes from one regime of value to another, creating the extraordinary distributions that we see today.

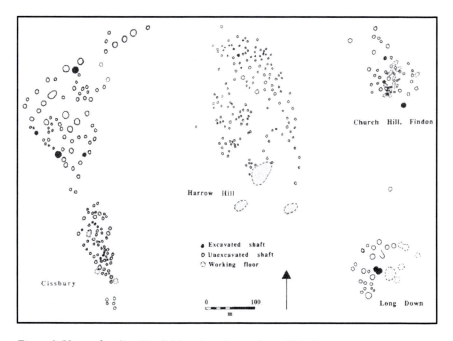

Figure 9 Plans of earlier Neolithic mines in southern Britain.

It may have been the associations of axes which conditioned their use in another important practice of the time. In a number of regions, people appear to have deliberately cast material into rivers. These deposits could include pottery and even fragments of human remains, but axes were a common element. Sometimes tied to protracted funerary rites, these acts of consumption may also have been gifts to the gods, prestations that bestowed honour on those who placed spirits in their debt. Inscribed with rich biographies, axes helped define relations between people and the ancestral world.

These were not entirely novel practices. Flaked axes were produced and perhaps circulated between people during the later Mesolithic. There are even a few ground stone axes in these earlier contexts. However, we should not downplay the change occasioned by the development of mines and quarries. These were monuments just as much as the first tombs and enclosures.

Under what circumstances were these sources encountered and used? So far as we can tell, the vast majority of mines and quarries were set apart from the main areas of contemporary settlement. Even though adequate raw material could often be found closer to home, prominent mountains or chalk hills developed as specific places to which people travelled to work stone. They involved a journey, and there may have been times when they were socially liminal; places where day-to-day norms were suspended or challenged. Some developed in woodland clearings while others lay close to grassland. Some involved walks of several days and a few at least were probably visited during the seasonal round of cattle husbandry. There is little evidence for fixed settlement in their environs and no indication that they were in continuous use by gangs of full-time specialists. Their use was essentially episodic or event-like, with working undertaken by small groups. Even in the case of the largest mine complexes, it seems likely that only a small number of shafts would have been open at any one time. The same is probably the case for the periodic camps established on the margins of upland quarries.

These characteristics have important consequences for our understanding of the purposes served by events at these sources. Often visible from a distance and sometimes dominating the skyline, these scarred mountains and hillsides 'altered the earth' just as much as major ceremonial monuments. For some, the use of a source involved a measure of temporary separation from the wider community. Undertaken as an adjunct to herding or hunting or for its own sake, a visit created the potential for distinctions to be made in terms of who was allowed to participate. Such distinctions may have been far from rigid and it is unwise to assume that they remained constant. Nevertheless, it is possible that this potential was realised in the definition of close kinship, in the reproduction of age grades and gender roles. At the same time, the capacity for axes to stand as tokens of identity was shaped – in part at least – by the creation of a space between the contexts in which they were produced and those in which they were carried and used. Embedded in broader routines of movement, activities at mines and quarries may have been keyed into conceptual schemes concerning patterns and thresholds in the lives of the individual, the community, and the broader social group. Beyond kinship, perhaps the reaching of a certain age brought with it access to the working floors that spread around the mouth of a shaft or the base of a quarry face. Perhaps it also brought access to stories about the past behind these places.

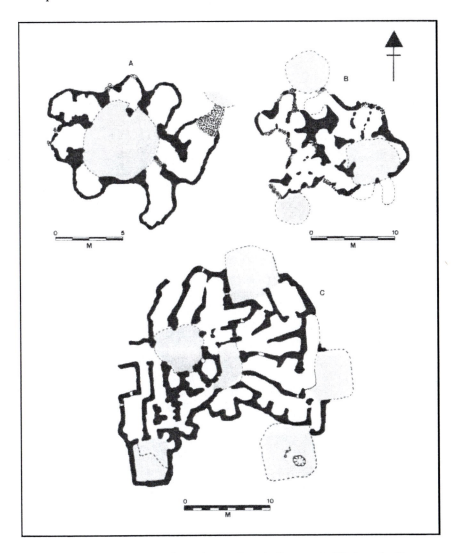

Figure 10 Shafts and galleries from three mines in Sussex. A: Blackpatch; B: Harrow Hill; C: Cissbury. 'Progress along the gallery is far from easy. One must crawl on elbows and stomach, trailing useless legs over hard and angular pieces of chalk, one's fingers spluttered with candle grease' (Curwen, 1934: 19).

The location of mines and quarries may have been of further significance where they were exploited by a range of people. Sources were not necessarily the preserve of close kin alone. It is more likely that they were exploited by members of different communities who were nonetheless linked by shifting ties of kinship and affiliation. Customary rights of access may have existed between groups and even between people and ancestral forces, and these would have to be addressed and renewed. On occasion, the mounting of a trip to a mine or quarry involved prior agreements, the discharging of obligations and perhaps the undertaking of various observances. Formal deposits, engravings and even human remains at certain mines suggest that these also took place on site. Under these circumstances, sources developed as settings in which a variety of meetings and transactions could be anticipated and undertaken.

How was working organised at particular sources? What can we say about the manner in which people worked in relation to the stone and to others? The practice of mining for flint or quarrying for stone was fraught with risks and uncertainties. Material might not be found at the bottom of a shaft and, even when it was, the properties of chalk made the winning of stone a protracted and potentially dangerous undertaking. At quarries, where fire was sometimes used to prepare and work the face, heating brought with it rockfalls and sudden splinters as well as the sighs and groans of fracturing rock. Perhaps these sounds were heard as the voices of the spirit caught within the stone. Sometimes balanced on the edge of high cliffs, some quarries were located so as to emphasise a sense of danger and separation. Often lost in our accounts is the drama that attended these events; the climbing and descending, the cracking of rock and the echoes, the vantage afforded by the climb. Just as the fires of quarrying camps would have been seen at a distance, so camps at a high quarry would have looked across wood and grass to the smoke trails of distant settlements.

At flint mines, the process of actually sinking a shaft would have been a group effort, requiring co-operation between a number of people. This would have also applied to the backfilling of shafts, which often took place once an episode of working had been completed. Although different in character, the firing of stone and the working of quarries at upland sources required similar arrangements. So far as we can tell, the bulk of the flint that was located during the sinking of the shaft and the working of narrow, radial galleries was taken up to the surface in a relatively unmodified state. Nests of waste flakes have been found in shafts, but it was at working areas on the surface that the creation of rough-out axes was generally undertaken. While galleries are absent on upland stone sources, individual quarries offer parallels with mine shafts – relatively bounded areas in which extraction was undertaken. Working floors are often found close by, or on camps established in the vicinity. Axe production dominates their inventories.

We can explain many of these characteristics in common-sense terms, emphasising the constraints imposed by the local geology and topography.

Figure 11 Earlier Neolithic mine at Harrow Hill (Sussex) under excavation. (Photo: courtesy of Worthing Museum.)

An account of these concerns does not, however, exhaust the significance that shafts and quarries may have had for those who worked and for those who watched. The layout of these sites provided a frame that structured the arrangement and movement of people. This provided cues for their understanding of the artefacts they produced and their relationships with others. Within the limits of a source, specific shafts and quarries were distinct and sometimes bounded entities. They demarcated areas within which work could be undertaken and they created the potential for distinctions to be drawn in terms of who could work with whom. Members of different communities may have come together to work at a particular shaft or quarry, or working may have been undertaken solely in the company of close kin. Travelling with the cattle for the first time, children could have watched and mimicked their elders, sometimes learning by instruction or rebuke. On this point at least, it is difficult to be certain, but working necessarily required close co-operation. The marking out of the shaft, the cutting of the chalk and the removal of flint involved physical contact and agreement. It was a group endeavour and a medium through which the ties that bound the group were acknowledged and carried forward. Similar ideas may have been evoked by the process of backfilling shafts. The customary conclusion to an episode of working – the restoring of the earth – brought proceedings to a close and, in that sense at least, it echoes some of the qualities that we commonly ascribe to rituals. Quarries have different characteristics but invite similar readings. Fire setting, where practised, involved a number of people and considerable skill. So too did the preparation and maintenance of a quarry face during working.

Having carried stone from a shaft or quarry to a working area, further scope existed for the evocation of ties between people, and between people and tools. Debris around shafts and quarries attests to the creation of working floors close to the place where stone had been obtained. These spreads of waste and rejected rough-outs suggest the persistent use of a particular location by a number of people working in close proximity. These were places where people sat, sometimes facing each other. Participants and audience would have been able to observe the production of axes by others, and would themselves have been observed. The fact that flaked axes were completed on these floors suggests that this pattern of working also confirmed an association between specific people and the artefacts they produced.

These intensive episodes of axe production also provided a context in which the skills of bifacial knapping could be watched and appreciated and, for some, learned and developed. Just as knowing how to test and quarter nodules, or how to set and tend a quarry fire required instruction and practice, so the working of stone in particular ways involved the watching of accustomed hands. Out of this process of instruction may have sprung distinctions that separated the skilled from the novice and the old from the young. What constituted a good blank? How did one turn the edge of a tool or rectify mistakes? What was the best angle from which to detach the thin, curved flakes that sprang from the hammer during the finishing of a rough-out? How could you use your body to cushion a blow? The basic answers to these questions are easy to recognise in the abstract, but in practice they take

Figure 12 Surface exposure of axe-making debris on an old working floor.

time to acknowledge and perfect. And as you learn, so you also hear stories of the past, of how things are, and of the world beyond your immediate horizons. Even at this intimate level, learning to work in particular ways involved an acknowledgement of social relations.

The practice of visiting and using important sources sustained a variety of social categories and this may have been the case with the working of other materials such as clay or plants. Just as they helped to mould the significance accorded to particular tools, so conventions surrounding the right to participate played their part in sustaining distinctions drawn on the basis of age and gender. At the same time, the actual practice of participation may have been crucial to the ways in which people acknowledged their position in broader networks of kinship, alliance and affiliation.

With the passing of generations, many sources loomed larger on the horizon, occupying more prominent positions in the biographies of communities. In addition to ancestral ties, these were places to which kin had come before. The maintenance of traditional patterns of working chalk, flint and

Figure 13 A stone axe quarry in the central Lakeland fells. Perched high on the face of the mountain, these precarious quarries were places to which people travelled to make tools that were also important tokens of identity and value.

other stone offered confirmation of the ties that bound the present to the past. As prominent landmarks, sources also came to stand as metaphors for the ties that stretched across the social landscape and between communities. Old features helped to guide new ventures and they served as tangible reminders of earlier events. Here was a hammer that had been used a few years ago; here was an old shaft and a scatter of debris that had always been there. These traces spoke of the roots that bound the present to the past and to the ancestors. Maintained in the shadow of old spoil heaps, traditional patterns of working brought those ties into focus through the rhetoric of re-enactment.

What was it that people took with them when they left these sites? Carried away from sources and back to the world of everyday activity, flaked axes and other tools carried associations with specific people and with the circumstances in which they were produced. These associations would have been strengthened through grinding and polishing, which was often undertaken within settlements. This enhanced the appearance and perhaps the recognisability of individual axes and may have added to their role as markers of identity. This process would not have ended there. With the passage of time, the day-to-day use and simple possession of these tools added a patina of routine associations. Tacit for much of the time, these biographies would have been drawn upon when axes were deployed in displays, in cycles of exchange, or in acts of formal deposition.

In addition to the artefacts themselves, people leaving a source carried other traces with them. First and foremost, there were the scars, cuts and other superficial injuries inevitably sustained during stoneworking. To these can be added the more chronic ailments that arise from a prolonged and repeated association with these activities, such as silicosis and emphysema. Where flintworking was a common practice, distinctive cuts and scars would

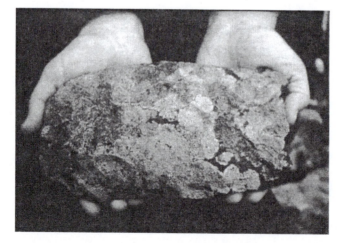

Figure 14

not have been exclusive to those who had worked stone at these places. The same is also true for other chronic ailments. However, for people returning from a trip to a source, cuts, scars and even respiratory problems may have confirmed their attendance and participation in these periodic events.

Chalk can be washed from the body and cuts and other injuries may heal and fade. What may have been of more profound significance were the techniques that were inculcated during episodes of intensive knapping at particular sources. Routine knowledge of different trimming or recovery techniques, of the best way to turn an edge, or of steps to be taken in maintaining a pattern of bifacial working. Much of this knowledge would have found its expression through the orientation of the body during work-ing, through the co-ordination of hands, and through other forms of gesture. The development of particular material repertoires would have also gone hand in hand with the capacity to speak knowledgeably about particular tasks and their associations. Like the techniques themselves, contributions to talk or discussion about working stone would have lent themselves to the structuring of basic principles of social classification within the community. They may seldom have been explicitly acknowledged, but the development of these skills played its part in shaping how people who had worked at sources were seen by kin and perhaps by others. Polished over time, stoneworking tech-nique held a metaphoric significance for the progression of a person through various stages in their life.

A hammer falling on stone creates echoes; sounds that change or fade with distance from the moment of working. Separated as we are by several thousand years and by very different attitudes towards technology, the echoes of earlier Neolithic stoneworking traditions are difficult to catch. That may be why we often treat the tools and tasks of the time as self-evident; products of a realm that we can comprehend through the applica-tion of common sense. If there is a general point to be drawn from this chapter, it is that such a response may be unwise. Our practical reason is not theirs and is itself a product of current values and historical circumstance. Things were different.

For contemporary communities, the collection and use of stone was as much a social fact as it was a response to practical problems. Different episodes or forms of stoneworking sustained values at several scales of social resolution. Patterns of procurement stretched across the land and across the seasons, bringing people into contact with both kin and non-kin. Choreographed by tradition, these routines were part of the way in which they renewed their commitment to particular places and their ties with others.

Set within these traditions were others that guided even the most intimate of gestures; ways of bringing a hand to stone, techniques for setting fire against a rock face. The subtle persuasion of particular forms of working was itself bound up in the definition of bonds and even in ways of thinking about the self. Above all else, people working stone in customary ways encountered the past through their actions. Traceable in the form of a hill or in the turn of a hand, other times were always present; the past of genealogies and of ancestral time itself. Held in tools and techniques handed down across generations, the dead and older spirits were a presence in even the most mundane spaces of people's lives.

6 A gift from the ancestors

They had started early, a dozen people on the trail keeping time with their stock. A skein of mist clung to the trees behind them in the valley; the breath of the cattle hung in the air on either side of their path. For three days they had walked from the lodge by the river, where pigs turned roots and meat dried in the smoke. It would have been two, but there had been a meeting with cousins from the next valley. The sharing of food and talk had added to the walk.

Sitting near the stock and charged with their tending, the children waited impatiently for sleep to arrive and for night to pass. Another night by the path, another night by the fire. Sharing food with the elders, they listened to plans for the days ahead, talk of signs along the way and of those they could expect to meet. When the dew caught the first light, they were the first to rise and rub the stiffness from their bones at what remained of the fire. This was their first time at the source.

The signs were good. The forest had fed them well and the cattle had not been tempted from their way by spirits. Old paths remained open and walking was easy. There were no arguments when they crossed the pastures of others, no feuds to be resolved. For once, the preparations had gone well.

It was not always so easy. Their grandfather had told them of a year when the earth would not give up its own. They had heard the story many times. It was his thirteenth summer and his second trip to the source. Ghosts in the trees conspired to hide the path in dense scrub. Wolves took a heifer on the first night and, by morning, the muttering had started. Perhaps the time was not right. Those who should have known better had lost the way. People became irritable. There had even been arguments over food usually shared without question and by the time the mines were reached, a few had followed their thoughts towards home.

Then it rained. Skies that had been bruised for days shed water that the earth would not swallow. The ground became heavy; chalk would not lift. It slipped from their hands and refused to leave the earth. After two days, the shaft was not much more than a hollow and no nodules had been found. It was on the second day that he fell. Straining to widen a fissure in the chalk, he lost his balance and fell against a block. The crack was heard by everyone; the breaking of a leg that was never true again. 'I heard an echo as it broke.' The words had become an incantation, mumbled under his breath whenever the way became hard or steep. After that, the mines had been abandoned. No stone was collected that time. Had it been found at all, it would have been weak from the frost that ached in his leg whenever autumn turned to winter. But things were different this time. The signs were good.

The mines had always been there. They had opened of their own accord, the ancestors giving themselves in the gift of flint. Stone for tools and stone for fire. The old ones were the children of the land and the land looked after them. All was well. The children were fat. But like all children, they began to take the gift for granted. They grew lazy and forgot how to return it through their working. Hands that had flashed with fire became dull. So the land turned its back, hiding the stone in its chalky frame. All that remained on the surface was the debris of those first days of working, remnants now in rivers or on the shoulders of low hills. The flint became a counter-gift; bestowed when the ancestors were honoured. The chalk would not open without their help. That was how it was.

The steady tempo of the path was broken when they arrived in the clearing around the mines. The sun had still some way to climb. The cattle paused. Uncertain where to graze, they began to break ranks, their feet following their tongues. Soon they were mingled with other stock. No one noticed. Their eyes were fixed on small knots of people and on mounds of weathered chalk that seemed larger than the oldest midden. Other kin had arrived three days before and there were shouts of recognition and calls to the fire. They had already begun to break the earth with antler and axe. Long, straight timbers had been cut and hardened in the hearths by which the old men sat. One shaft was open and out of the chalk came the muffled cries of those who laboured in the galleries below. Shouts for assistance and more light; the crack of heavy nodules being quartered before lifting; curses when the sharp stone bit back. There would be help needed before another shaft was opened, but that was good. The hard work here had already been done.

Within hours, talk which had ranged from one family to another became more focussed. Greetings and gossip gave way to plans. Squatting near the fire, the older men deliberated on where the new shaft would go and on where old galleries were to be avoided. The children heard of shafts dug many years before, their backfill now concealed beneath coarse grasses. They heard of the old times, when the good stone lay close to the surface. Names they remembered and names that were new. As plans turned to stories, they learned of the stonechats who lived at the mines. To hear one was a blessing, for the birds were spirits. Their percussive song was an echo of the first hammer on the first stone. That was how it was. Some of the women laughed. What if the men used their strength in digging and not in talking? That was also how it was when there was work to be done. Laughter cut the knot around the fire and discussion came to a close.

Work began. A chain of hands received the quartered nodules as they were pulled from the shaft. Inserting himself in the line, one of the boys took his turn, receiving the stone from his sister. Careful to keep the sharp, black meat of the flint away from his arms, he passed the block to a cousin he had not seen since his initiation. There would be other stories to hear later on. The younger boy could not carry stone with the ease or pace of his elders. He stood to one side, peering into the shaft and jumping out of the way until he learned the pattern of the work. Seen from above, the bodies of those in the galleries took on the colour of old bones. Smeared with a rime of chalk and clay, they crawled out of the dark tugging ropes they had wound around the floorstone.

Sometimes the birth was easy. Nodules slid across the greasy chalk and emerged into the light to be quartered. At other times, the belly of the earth would not be relieved of its burden so readily. A figure would disappear back into a gallery to help in the labour and those in the shaft would fall silent. This was when rockfalls were most likely and ears were set for the creak of moving chalk. Only when the figure reappeared would talk and encouragement begin again.

Up above, the sound of nodules being turned and tested gradually gave way to the rhythms of flaking. Squatting next to his uncle, the older boy watched as the others brought axes and cores out of the stone. Taking a small hammer from his bag, he bent forward and picked up a flake. His uncle shook his head and pointed to the fault that ran through the stone. He leant over and tapped it with his hammer. It gave a dull crack and split along the fault. An ugly break, one that would not take an edge. There were a few laughs and the boy discarded the broken flake for the piece his uncle offered him.

Turning the stone in one hand as the others did, he found a balance and a purchase and began to work. Hesitant at first, flaking became easier once the skin of the flint had gone. Working one face then the other, the boy reduced the mass of the stone. This was the easy part. Everyone could work stone in this way. It was once the rough shape of the axe had been achieved that the task began in earnest.

The boy was nervous. He had made axes before, but never here, and not with the good stone. Like his brothers and sisters, he had learned to work with the flint from the river of his birth. This was different. The stone in his hand was a part of the ancestors and bad working showed disrespect.

Pressing the stone against his leg, he used a worn antler tine to deliver shallow blows to the edge. The soft report of the hammer was followed by the clatter of a large flake as it was brushed to the ground. A thin scar sent ripples across the face of the axe just as he had hoped. The blow had not bitten too deep. Turning the axe with each blow, he repeated the action, working his way around the edge and changing tack when needed. He no longer heard the work and the talk around him. He did not notice the blood on his hands where the edge had caught the skin. It did not matter; the cuts were slight. They would be thin lines by morning and lost among other scars within a few days.

The task progressed. Where once he had merely dressed the stone, now the boy took care to trim only where necessary. Mistakes at this late stage brought curses from even the most patient. Blows became lighter; more considered. The antler dropped with its own weight and none of his making; all he had to do was determine where it fell.

His uncle touched his arm and made him pause. You had to know when to stop; when to put the hammer down and step back. There were murmurs of approval in the circle. 'Not bad. . . . A smooth face and a sharp line to help in the grinding. . . . He'll be good one day.' Brushing the dust from his body, the boy sat back from the bed of shattered stone that had gathered below his knees.

His hands became familiar with the axe as he watched the others work, sometimes glancing down at the thin ridge of cortex that ran along the spine. He had failed to remove the last of the skin. It annoyed him at first but, again, it did not matter. There would be days of grinding and polishing before the task was finished. He would be home before the haft was cut and cured. By then, the skin would be gone. This was an axe that he would keep. He would polish it until it shone, grinding and regrinding the edge to keep it keen. With luck, it would rest across his shoulder for many years. It would grow old, diminish alongside him.

He listened to the older men as their hammers danced and coaxed long flakes from the stone. It went so fast that he wondered how they managed to talk while they worked. Yet talk they did, turning their heads from time to time to cough and spit the rattle from their chests. Which tools would be kept and which would be traded? When was the next gathering which would bring the clan together? Why had so many cattle died last winter? By the time the shadows had reached the edge of the working floor, most had a handful of tools and cores at their side. All had caught up on events since they had last sat together.

There would be more work the next day and for nine after that, though the pace was slow and the roll-call varied. Time spent in eating and talking, in collecting food and watching stock. Some returned to the forest to hunt with their cousins for a day. Some slipped away for other reasons. There would be deals struck, marriages discussed and celebrations planned. Only when it came to restoring the earth would everyone gather again among the broken stone. Offerings would be made to give thanks for the gift they had received: food for the earth in a simple bowl, tools that had splintered and cracked in the vice of the chalk. The chain would form again, this time carrying chalk and hides of rubble back to the edge and down to the floor. After that there would be dancing and the gleam of fat on faces by the fire. More stories. More boasts. More laughter. And then the time to part; the return to winter clearings. Feet in step with hooves and opportunities for trade along the way. The moon would be full by the time they saw the river and they would have much to tell the others.

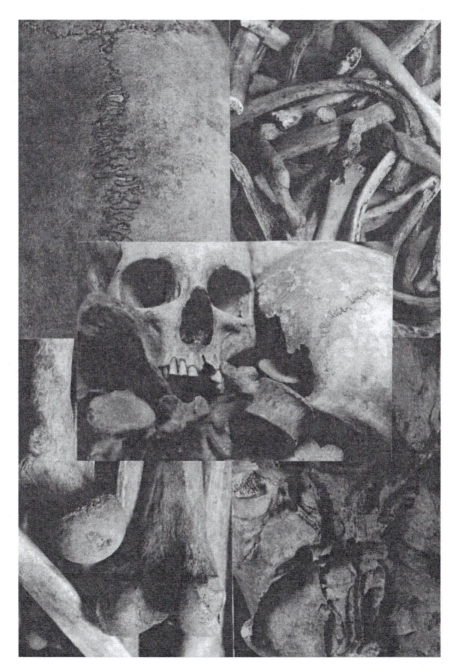

Figure 15

7 The living and the dead

Walk along the Ridgeway south-west from Uffington. Keep the White Horse behind you, Dragon Hill and the Vale over your right shoulder. Half an hour or so will bring you to Wayland's Smithy, an earlier Neolithic tomb within a perimeter of tall beeches. The name handed down from a time when metalworking was remembered as a potent, even magical, practice, the site is a long trapezoidal mound with a transepted endchamber. A line of tall sarsens provide an impressive facade, their surfaces pitted and hollowed by erosion. Stone kerbs can be traced on either side, and the mound is flanked by chalk-cut ditches that have lost their definition under centuries of silting.

A small island in a sea of arable, the tomb lies on the threshold between lowland and upland. It is also on the path that runs along the crest of the downs, a path that may have been used during prehistory. Nowadays it is visited by walkers, though it has seen recent use for 'pagan' rites, private observance and seasonal parties. Amongst the leaves that cover the floor of the chamber each autumn, it is common to find candles, flowers, the smell of incense and stale urine. Often there are coins lying in the hollows of the sarsens, offerings made for luck or perhaps to wake the smith who once shod horses overnight. Nobody leaves horses any more, nor have they for centuries. The offerings are romance, nostalgia for a past that exists in the modern imagination and in reactions to the present.

Visiting Wayland's Smithy today, it is easy to believe that the monument is a singular entity. Scheduled and maintained for a future as yet unspecified, it appears stable, as if it was a building designed and executed in a single episode. Appearances can be deceptive. Excavation has revealed a far more complex history caught up in this place, a sequence of events and phases, of modelling, remodelling and elaboration over time. The line began with the stripping of turf, the clearing of ground and the laying down of an area of sarsen paving. Flanked by boulders and posts, this area was the focus for deposits of human remains; a crouched body and the disarticulated remnants of some fifteen others. At least one child is present and there are hints of exhumation and perhaps the removal of individual bones. Some of the bones have been gnawed by animals and there were three broken leaf-shaped arrowheads, each in close contact with a human pelvis. Fronted by an arrangement of

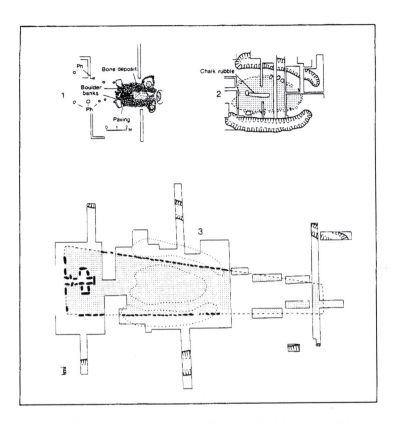

Figure 16 The structural sequence at Wayland's Smithy, Oxfordshire (after Kinnes 1992).

substantial posts, it is unclear how long the monument stood in this form. In that time, people probably visited more than once, perhaps bringing new bones or bodies and taking old deposits away. These visits may have also brought additions to the rubble banks and timber settings and, while we cannot be certain, it may be that this continued for a handful of generations.

With time, the pattern of events involved more profound changes. Access to certain deposits was denied by the infilling of the earlier chamber with chalk rubble. This, in turn, was followed by the cutting of flanking ditches and the raising of a mound of chalk and earth while some of the earlier timbers were still standing. Bracketed by the ditches, the mound was embellished with a few sarsen boulders to create a simple forecourt. Shards of pottery and fragments of polished flint axes were found in the vicinity. The sequence continued. Again, it is difficult to specify the time period involved, but enough time had passed for scrub to regenerate in the immediate area. The entire mound and parts of the ditches were reworked by the addition of the more massive structure that dominates the place today. Flanked by yet larger ditches, the trapezoidal mound with its kerb, facade and endchamber absorbed the older mound altogether.

The evidence from Wayland's Smithy is better than that from many long mounds. Yet there is much we cannot say about the site, or the significance it held for those who participated in building and other rites at the time. The sequence suggests the labour of a relatively small company spread out across generations. It speaks of changes in the configuration of the monument, in the relation it had to the dead and its meanings for the living. Both the location of the mound and the character of the bones it seals also hint that this was a place that was visited, a place of periodic observance for the living, a house through which the dead might pass.

Living with the dead

A sense of ancestry was caught up in the routines that people followed. It could be brought into focus in a clearing, at a long-known stone source or in stories around a hearth. It informed people's knowledge of how to go on, lending a timeless quality to the tasks that turned on the seasonal round. This is how it is; it has always been this way. There were also occasions when that focus was sharper still. There were times and places when the ties between present and past became objects of discourse in their own right. Nowhere were these ties more clearly realised than at the tombs which begin to appear in the centuries around 4000 BC.

There were many ways of dying. There were good deaths and bad, there was death out of place, and the dead were an important presence in the land. Earlier generations imposed themselves upon the consciousness of the living. Tombs were often used to harness human remains, but fragments of bodies are

Figure 17 Facade at Wayland's Smithy.

found in many settings, suggesting that bones were also relics that circulated. Placed in pits they might speak of the ties that bound a community to an earlier generation and to a place where kin had lived before. Held and displayed during important gatherings they offered evidence of the rights and responsibilities that had been handed down from one generation to another. Cult objects handled by a shaman, they could be a medium for communication with other worlds. There were also the older ways of honouring the dead, ones that seldom leave an archaeological signature. The dispersal of bones or ashes in the forest of one's birth, the scattering of remains in rivers and perhaps even the consumption of flesh by animals. There were many paths along which people could pass into the ancestral world. Situated on some of these paths were the places like Wayland's Smithy that we now recognise as tombs.

Tombs were the houses of the ancestors. Responsible for the creation of the land and caught up in its fabric, they had the power to protect and influence the fortunes of the living. But what were tombs for? How were they implicated in the playing out of relations between people? Inevitably, there can be no single answer to these questions. Regional differences can be seen in the forms and histories of these sites, in their architecture and in the treatment accorded to human remains. In other words, we are dealing with variations on themes drawn upon differently from one region, one valley system and perhaps even from one generation to another. In the west, the earliest sites were often stone-built and include portal dolmens and rotunda graves. There are also simple passage graves whose distribution extends up to northern Scotland. In other parts of the country, early tombs were often made from arrangements of earth and timber. Sometimes, as at Streethouse in Cleveland, they took the form of a limited, rectangular area bounded by low banks of stone and earth or by freestanding timbers. Further variations on this theme may include long rectilinear mortuary enclosures such as Barford, Rivenhall or North Stoke. At Nutbane, Fussell's Lodge or Willerby Wold, timbers were also used to construct elaborate mortuary structures. Often approached via a forecourt or timber facade, these bounded areas provided the focus for linear arrangements of features, bodies, bones and other materials.

Visited over generations, many sites were remodelled through the addition of banks of earth or stone. These more monumental long barrows and long cairns often buried the traces of earlier activity and were themselves reworked over time. At Haddenham in Cambridgeshire, rough-hewn timbers formed a mortuary structure fronted by a ditch, bank and paved area. Only later was a substantial turf mound added to the site. This repeats a pattern seen elsewhere. Rising to a height of several metres, the imposing qualities of some of these mounds were enhanced where they were flanked by quarry ditches or by areas stripped of turf. Forms include the chambered trapezoidal cairns of the Cotswold–Severn area, the terminal chambered tombs around the Medway in Kent and the varied earthen mounds of Wessex and Yorkshire. Regional groupings and local traditions.

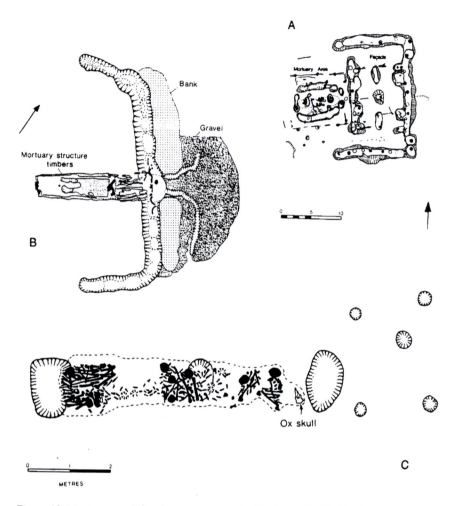

Figure 18 Mortuary and facade structures at A. Nutbane; B. Haddenham.
C. Mortuary deposits at Fussell's Lodge (after Kinnes 1992).

What significance did the living attach to the dead at these places? Patterns in the character of deposits suggest that tombs were caught up in complex rites of passage. In some areas, bodies or elements arrived already stripped of their flesh. Exposed or defleshed elsewhere, human bones were often brought to tombs to rest among the remains of earlier generations. That journey might take months, perhaps even years, bones being brought from pits or high points where they had rotted for some time. This seems to have been the case at sites like Ascott under Wychwood, where some of the interred bones show signs of prior exposure. In other cases, the tomb itself might be the place where flesh was corrupted. Bodies could be placed inside an entrance soon after death; slumped corpses slowly rotting in a prone or seated position as at Hetty Pegler's Tump. With that decay came the reordering, trampling and the removal of different skeletal elements. The stacking of limbs and skulls and even the reassembly of bodies with elements drawn from different people. These privileges may not always have been open to all. Bones could be taken from many tombs for deposition elsewhere or to circulate among the living. Within their bounds, however, it was a commonplace that the broken remains of a person were incorporated with the remnants of those long dead. Sometimes tombs could remain open and accessible, impediments to entry taking the form of spiritual danger alone. This is a tradition that we can trace in chambered tombs in the Cotswolds. In other cases, deposits might be sealed after an interval, with fires set across the bones before they were buried by earth and rubble. Expressions of this practice can be seen in a number of mounds in Yorkshire.

It is in the common emphasis on the collective over the individual that we can trace a concern with ancestral forces. These communities of bones contained kin who were remembered and mourned. But the customary breaking and reordering of their bodies suggests a desire to see the dead pass on into the ancestral realm, a realm which bound the community of the living to earlier generations. Few were singled out for special treatment within these sites, and there is only limited evidence for the provision of grave goods with specific people.

Here we must exercise a measure of caution. Tombs were implicated in rites of passage that took people from the world of the living to the ancestral realm. They could be places through which remains passed as the body and the spirit were transformed. Yet there are mounds that were raised without a deposit of human bone, or examples where those deposits seem no more than tokens. Sites like Beckhampton Road or South Street, where chalk mounds were raised over complex timber and hurdle settings but where the remains of people were absent. The significance of ancestral houses did not always rest upon the presence of dead kin. There were the prior histories attached to the land on which they stood, the land that they became a part of with time. Then there was the act of construction itself; the clearing of ground, the digging of ditches and the bringing together of timber, stone and earth, wood coppiced by an earlier generation, stone dragged from a more distant source or from an ancient sacred site. This was the labouring of people with a common vision of their relation to the past and to the land around them.

What was important was that tombs endured. They persisted in ways that the immediate trappings of many settlements did not. Massive timbers might outlive a generation and stone itself appeared to withstand time. Because of their persistence, tombs confronted the living with the broader continuum in which their lives unfolded. Through them people addressed the ties that bound them to the past. Shrouded in myth and perhaps watched over by spirits, these were places to which communities returned on many occasions. Sometimes that return brought fragments of the newly deceased, but often visits were as much in step with seasonal and ancestral rites as they were with the demise of a specific person. Entire groups may have gathered in the shadow of their ancestors at certain times. At others, attendance and observance may have been the privilege of only a few.

People wove a constellation of meanings and histories into these houses. Like a church of the Middle Ages, they were places where personal loss could be acknowledged and where a sense of kinship and community could be

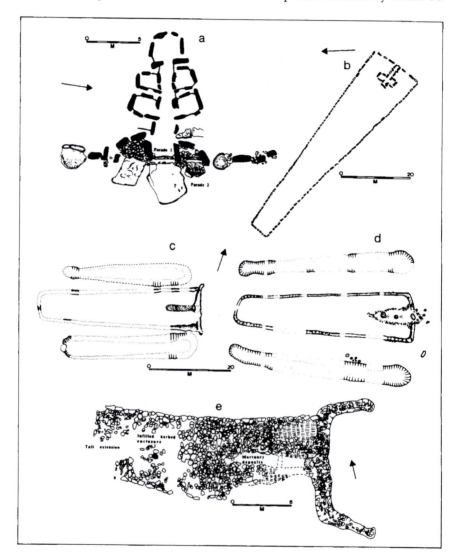

Figure 19 Earlier Neolithic mortuary sites. a. facade and burial chambers at
a. West Kennet; b. Wayland's Smithy; c. Willerby Wold; d. Fussell's Lodge;
e. Streethouse.

grounded in an ancestral and cosmological order. Important events at tombs could even implicate cycles and histories mapped out across the sky. Drawing attention to the rising and setting of the sun at midwinter or midsummer, the orientation of certain tombs linked the sky to the land and the seasonal round to myths of the longer term. Walking up to a tomb along a familiar path could also reveal that the moon rose or fell directly above, and this added to the gravity that attended particular events. Perhaps there were times when these shorter cycles took on a metaphoric significance for cycles in the lives of women. Associated with powerful forces, tombs were places to which people came to ask for intervention and support: women conducting rites of passage, men asking for help with the herd, the elders instructing a young initiate. As such, they were contexts where some might come to hold a local authority over others. Proximity to the ancestors was an index of the standing of particular people. The right to officiate could be the prerogative of family heads or of shamen and there were times when access to the forecourts or interior of tombs was restricted to only a few. Out of these distinctions came a sense of the order of relations among the living, an order which seemed all the more inevitable where its roots could be traced into the ancestral past.

The communities of bones that lay within could play an immediate and important part in this process. Inclusion may have often been a privilege of kinship and position and, once inside, the placement and reordering of bone may have brought certain values into sharp relief. The confusion of disarticulated and decaying remains could be read as a metaphor for the collective bonds of kinship and this has been a common theme in interpretation. Associated with specific lineages or small clusters of kin, tombs provided a model for the links that bound communities together. At times, this sense of commonality may have been more fictive than real. A rite which brought with it a sense of levelling in death could conceal differences of authority and fortune. We can only guess that these divisions respected marriage, descent and ties that stretched beyond the clearings of a few extended families. Where relations between people could shift with time and through the pursuit of political agendas, tensions would have condensed around these powerful places.

These frames were also used to idealise more basic distinctions. Sometimes the bones of the elders and of children were separated, drawing attention to the authority that set one generation apart from another. At Nympsfield, for example, this division was sustained through the placement of the cremated remains of children in a separate cist. Women could also be distinguished from men, a practice recognised at sites such as Lanhill and Notgrove. These distinctions were brought into focus as people handled and ordered skeletal remains; rites which involved the telling of stories about the ancestral past and the lives of earlier generations. Narratives may have even taken cues from the architecture of the tombs themselves. Where possible at all, entering a tomb was a dramatic and even dangerous event. Access may again have been a privilege of kinship or position. It involved crawling across the scattered remains of people, the smell of decay and glimpses of stacked skulls or limbs in the half-light. There were the bones of those who had never passed the threshold into adulthood and deep in the interior were the remains of the elders, some so old that their names had been forgotten or invented. The arrangement of chambers and deposits lent an order to the encounter people had with these relics. It was a model of relations among the living that could be manipulated or placed beyond question. Death brought changes in ties of kinship and authority. It threatened the continuity of the social order. It required the handing on of rights and responsibilities and these would be brought into focus at tombs. Seasonal rites also involved speaking to and on behalf of the ancestors. As a community gathered in the spring to seek help in the regeneration of seed corn, a forecourt emphasised the place in which only a few could stand and speak. Visited in late summer by cattle and close kin, a facade meant acknowledging the authority of those who could say what histories lay within. The position of elders or even of shamen was bound up in the right to mediate in ancestral rites, to know the histories attached to a place. To have the ear of these powerful forces was to have a certain standing.

We glimpse traces of these varied rites in material associations. Burials of cattle in the interior of some tombs suggest a close identification of people with their herds. Animal bone in ditches or features around these sites suggest limited gatherings and consumption in the company of ancestors. The eating of pork was often an important element in these events, the culmination of a feast sometimes marked by the deposition of food remains and pottery or the

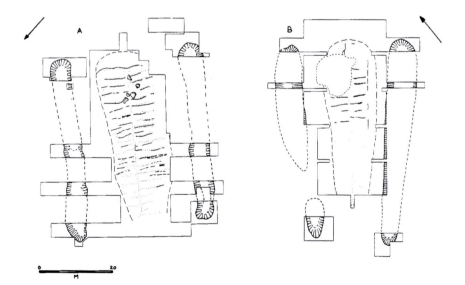

Figure 20 A. South Street, Wiltshire; B. Beckhampton Road, Wiltshire (after Kinnes 1992).

accumulation of midden. At sites like Fussell's Lodge and Hanging Grimston, debris in the forecourt area is consistent with the deliberate smashing of pots, a gesture that might be interpreted as an act of closure to an important event. At other times, people may have come in company or alone; to make offerings, to seek help or revelation. Returning at a later season, cleaning a ditch or gathered in a forecourt, they encountered this material as evidence for the past that attended these places. Here was a midden first established by the founders of a lineage: there were the fragments of vessels that had once contained offerings to the dead or food shared among kin. Events and past relations were made secure in social memory through these encounters. They were reconciled with the present.

In a landscape composed of places and paths, how did people come to tombs? Events conducted at these sites had important consequences for relations among those who participated. They might be regarded differently by those who were excluded, or by those who could only stand and watch. But the significance of tombs went beyond the remains of the dead, and this returns us to the broader routines in which those encounters were set. The settings of tombs are varied in the extreme. Some lay close to winter settlements, others in places occupied at different seasons and in other ways. Many are found in prominent locations, such as valley heads, false crests or ridge tops and likely paths of access. The chambered tomb at Nympsfield sits on the edge of the scarp above the Severn Valley, a pattern repeated elsewhere in the area. West Kennett near Avebury is also elevated, as are many mounds in Yorkshire or cairns like Minninglow in the Peak District. In North Dorset, several long mounds lay close to seasonal pastures and to sources of stone. A link with the pastures of late summer was strong in many areas. Often there was a close play with local topography. Some would be visible at a distance, yet hidden when close at hand, only revealed by the final climb. Approached from below, they could stand out on the skyline and provide a vantage from which to look out across the woods and clearings of familiar country. They could be passed and visited on a seasonal basis by others moving stock or travelling to collect stone.

Others were founded in more low-lying settings, equivalents for the long mortuary enclosures sometimes found on the gravel terraces of river valleys. They could be established in small clearings, on turf, or on earth that had been cultivated generations before. A number seal traces of later Mesolithic or earlier Neolithic settlement; sites like Kilham, Haddenham or South Street. Often they were founded in places that had specific cultural histories. Tombs in certain areas even drew attention to dramatic natural features – rivers and rocks or the peaks of prominent hills. This might be achieved through close association, so that a cairn or barrow could seem part of the earth itself. It might also come from the orientation of the body and the eye during the approach to a site. In some places at least, the gaze along the spine of a tomb directed attention to mythic or historic features – the rivers from which the first people had sprung or the hills that marked where they had once lived and

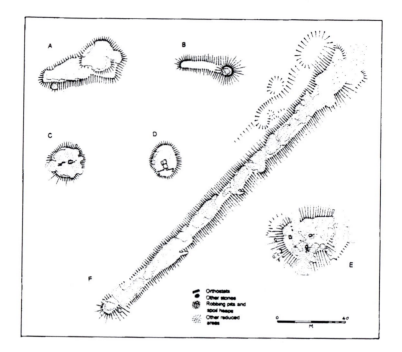

Figure 21 Tombs in the Derbyshire Peak District (after Barnatt 1996). Many of these places saw use, reuse and reinvention over considerable periods of time. In some cases, this was marked by remodelling or the addition of new mounds in the later Neolithic and Early Bronze Age. A. Long barrow with superimposed round barrow at Perryfoot. B. Long barrow with superimposed round barrow at Longstone Moor. C. Five Wells chambered barrow. D. Green Low chambered barrow. E. Minninglow. F. Chambered bank barrow at Long Low.

worked. Simply knowing the stories that they held may have been a function of age and initiation.

We could dismiss these patterns as coincidences, but a more common response is to cast these sites as territorial markers, statements of property rights made by particular communities. This idea seems to make sense to us, but actually it says very little. It implies a commonality of meaning and intent and misses the dramatic reworking of the significance of a place that the foundation of a tomb established. An old camp or clearing, a patch of grazing or an area visited by generations of hunters and herders now had ancestral occupants. These were forces to be respected and perhaps even feared. Where those involved in the foundation of a tomb were bound by ties of blood, the housing of the ancestors attached them to the land and to each other. This was as much a technology of kinship as it was a message to others. This attachment grew out of a cyclical pattern of life that often took people to and from these places. Visited at key junctures and seen or passed in the course of the seasonal round, the foundation and use of tombs was a potent medium through which people renewed a sense of tenure and belonging. Returning again and again and adding to the fabric and the content of tombs, they grounded that attachment in the ancestral past and projected it into the future.

Changing landscapes

We have followed a few of the contours of the earlier Neolithic, encountering some of the traditions that animated people's lives. We have visited scatters, tombs and different tasks and, as in the Neolithic, we shall return to these again. Yet before we take that path we must ask a more basic question. Why do we see the changes that we do? It is not enough to appeal to our own common sense. We should resist a tendency to make these landscapes too familiar. So how should we account for the appearance of new artefacts, the building of tombs and the use of domesticates themselves? One solution would be to look elsewhere and to envisage new people arriving from the continent. This was once a common response. Scholars in the first half of this century saw parallels in materials on either side of the channel and in them the signature of colonisation. Similar pots meant similar people and accounts often emphasised large migrations as prime movers in economic and social change.

Although this remains an accepted view for some, more recent work has pulled many back from this position. We now recognise that the timescale over which these processes unfolded was far longer than originally appreciated. We also accept that artefacts and ideas can move independently of people in the playing out of local concerns. Cross-channel contact was a reality in certain regions. It is a modern conceit that the sea was the barrier that it symbolises for many today. With that contact came an encounter with new materials and ideas, a continual reworking of ties of kinship, alliance and exchange. However, this was a localised ebb and flow of people, not a grand wave of advance. Much of what we see reflects change brought about through the agency of indigenous communities. This position may be a product of modern political geographies, just as a concern with the roots of twentieth-century ethnicities can be traced in talk of migrations. Whatever the case, there remains the issue of why we see the changes that we do.

For some, the appearance of pottery, polished tools and monuments is regarded as an inevitable by-product of food production. Farming brought with it new concerns and the surplus required to engage in activities such as monument building. For others, the Neolithic was something that happened 'in the mind as much as the ploughsoil'. It involved the introduction of a new 'blueprint' for thinking about the self and society, a new symbolic order which set the wild against the tame. There are important points in both of these arguments. Yet what is often lost is the scale and diversity of what we call the 'Mesolithic/Neolithic transition' as it was lived and experienced. For people at the time, there would have been no transition, no threshold across which the world changed, just a piecemeal recruitment of new ideas and resources at local, dispersed scales.

The landscapes of southern Britain had been inhabited by hunters and collectors since their time began, people bound by webs of social relations and by connections with particular places and paths. Their lives had long been animated by a concern with the fertility of nature and of people, the cycles and histories of the land and their ties with others. Distinctions between women and men, the elders and their subordinates and between kin and non-kin did not arrive with the first domesticates. Nor did questions of tenure, affiliation or renown. They had been important for many generations. What happened over time was a reworking of the practices through which people understood and addressed these issues.

This process had a fragmented quality which is lost when we talk of prime movers or blueprints. Season to season and generation to generation, questions of tenure, identity and authority were addressed with reference to new material and symbolic resources. The herding of cattle, the control of ancestors and the provision of labour, all provided media through which relations between people could be carried forward. Rooted and reworked from an ethic of sharing that is common among gatherers and hunters, the giving of new gifts was itself caught up in this process. New ways of working stone offered different potentials for the definition of identities and for exchange. So too did domesticates, the use of sickles or laurel leaves; the display and circulation of fine axes or arrows. The production and possession of these tools spoke of the qualities and biographies of people. They were 'good to think with' as well as good to use. Some, of course, were even used in graded combat, a practice in which identity and renown might be crucial. In a similar way, pottery involved new attitudes towards the preparation, consumption and sharing of food. Earth transformed by fire, pots and their contents could also be passed as good or gift and this contributed to their use in ceremonies and other events. Like other tools, they could serve as tokens of identity and value; in their forms could be held the history of relations between people.

Reworked over time and in different ways from one region to another, this piecemeal process brought with it changes in the land that were no less profound for being unforeseen. The working of ties between people, land and the past set up new rhythms and raised concerns that were as much ecology as they were politics. New ways of thinking about the self and society brought changes in material traditions, in the configuration of the land and in the character and season of its use. Cattle grazed on summer pastures that had long been visited for game; settlements and gardens were founded where more transient camps had stood before. And with pastures and plots came a new relationship between past, present and future. Stock and crops were a legacy bestowed upon the next generation. Those who tended gardens or followed their herds owed a debt to those who had gone before. The continuity of life not only required co-operation between the living and the ancestors, but also involved a responsibility that stretched across the years and between generations. Sustained in a different manner to the resources of the wild, herds, pastures, crops and gardens engendered a different sense of tenure.

It is against such a background that we should consider the foundation and development of tombs. Tombs fixed the ancestors of a community to land that had once been passed or used by others. They redefined the traditional associations of the places and paths on which they were founded. Encountered in the course of annual cycles of movement and activity, their use gave expression to ties of kinship and community. Gathered in the company of the ghosts of the past and seeking help in the continuation of life, communities acknowledged the debt that they owed to earlier generations. But like the keeping of stock or the circulation of new gifts, the ancestral rites that emerged in the early fourth millennium held a potential for change. They were sources of symbolic capital and, as such, they could be recruited in the pursuit of sectional interests.

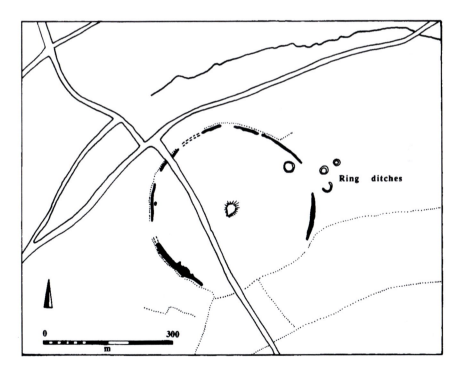

Figure 22 Outline plan of the great barrow and surrounding enclosure at Duggleby Howe, Yorkshire (after Kinnes *et al.* 1983). Excavated in the nineteenth century we know little about the relationship between the two. We cannot tell if the circle was cut to contain the dead, or whether they were added to an older arena.

Ancestral houses were reworked with time. Begun as free-standing and diminutive structures, many became more monumental. They were embellished through the addition of earth or stone, the extension of mounds, or the construction of more elaborate facades, palisades and revetments. Sites like Tilshead Old Ditch saw the swallowing of the original mound in a more massive chalk-bank. Others were extended by substantial tails that more than doubled their length. This concern was also addressed through the incorporation of tombs into cursus monuments. Here they could become important reference points for those participating in important processions or those permitted to see the sun rise and set within their banks. This finds a vivid expression on Cranborne Chase in Dorset and on the gravels at Dorchester-on-Thames.

Many chambered tombs were also elaborated, becoming the dramatic monuments that we see today. An ancient site of collective burial might be incorporated in a new cairn, the bones of the old ones brought into new associations with the remains of those who had died more recently. New chambers or deposits might bring the dead of different families together in novel arrangements, signifying shifts in fortune and authority among the living. Perhaps there were even times when long-forgotten or contested mounds were harnessed in different genealogies or given new names in stories of the ancestral past. Recruited by the living, ancestral houses could confirm a sense of continuity between present and past where none had been before. This is our house; we know the names of those it holds, and the times and places of their lives.

Changes in outward appearance went hand in hand with other shifts of emphasis. Over the course of the earlier Neolithic, there were further developments in the character of many tombs. Prominent among these was the degree of access that people had to the relics these houses contained. Tombs that had long been open began to be sealed up, sometimes by facades. A dramatic backdrop against which to speak, these facades sealed ancestral remains and limited the possibility of their removal or manipulation. Although many sites continued to be a focus for varied rites, events now turned directly upon those with the capacity to speak on behalf of the ancestors; to intercede between the living and the dead.

There were other changes too. The extent to which communities in different areas practised collective burial and the disarticulation of remains had always been varied. Relics still circulated. But with the passage of time there was a falling away of this tradition, particularly in areas such as the Thames Valley and Yorkshire. New mounds were constructed, sometimes within circuits of ditched enclosures, but as with the later deposits in some chambered tombs, these were often built to seal a few articulated bodies. Sites like Radley near Abingdon saw the throwing up of a gravel mound over the crouched burials of both a man and a woman. Associated with these bodies was a belt fitting made of jet and a long flint blade with a polished edge. Although burial prevented further contact with the bodies, the site continued

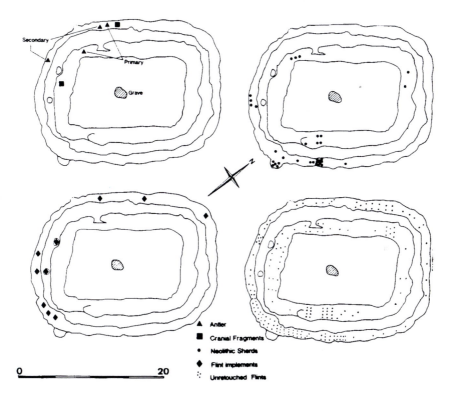

Figure 23 Plan of the double-ditched barrow at Barrow Hills, constructed on the
margins of a causewayed enclosure near Abingdon (after Bradley 1992).
Originally a ditched enclosure, the site gradually developed into a barrow
with additional ditch circuits. The south-western end of the site remained
open at certain times: two large posts flank this 'approach' to the area of the
grave, and it is possible that other posts in the ditches formed a facade at
this end of the site. Spatial patterning suggests that animal bone, stone tools
and fragmentary human remains were deliberately placed in the ditches
close to this entrance, their resting places marked by posts. Other details of
the patterning reflect the continued importance of this area in front of the
barrow as a focus for activities which may have included feasts.

to be a focus for signal events; the cutting of enclosing ditches, episodes of
consumption and acts of deposition. At Whitegrounds in Yorkshire, a cairn
constructed over a linear arrangement of disarticulated remains was reworked.
The cairn was enlarged and a grave cut into the heart of the mound. Here the
body of a young man was placed on his side, accompanied in death by an axe
and a flint blade. A similar belt fitting to that found at Radley suggests that the
body was clothed.

What do these various changes signify? Here again, there is much that we
cannot know and little basis for generalisation. Sequences and histories vary.
Those histories do, however, hint at changes in the relationship between the

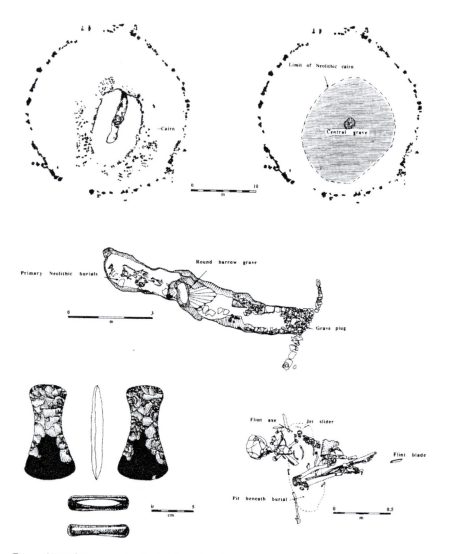

Figure 24 Whitegrounds, Yorkshire. The first phase at this site saw disarticulated
    human remains placed in a grave beneath a low cairn. After an interval of
    time the site was reused, becoming the focus for the articulated burial of a
    man with a polished jet belt slider and a distinctive 'Seamer' axe.

living and the ancestors. Closure suggests that some took on a greater
responsibility as mediators, a role that brought with it a certain authority.
Increased monumentality may indicate a greater concern with displaying the
strength of the ties that bound people to place, to themselves and perhaps to
others. Scale might be taken as a sign of duration. The rhetoric of scale could
also be directed towards other issues. Imposing cursus monuments reflect the

labour of many and suggest a concern with a rather broader collective. Like causewayed enclosures, they hint at regional social identities that stretched beyond the boundaries of close kinship. Constructed and elaborated over generations, the ancestral rites and gatherings that these places witnessed had consequences for many. Where lineage heads or shamen held sway and others listened to talk of the past, a long mound on the skyline or in the fabric of a processional way gave a sense of deep roots behind the present order of things.

The treatment of the body was also crucial. Emphasis had once been placed upon the collective, but burial now drew more attention to specific people; relatives with roles and biographies held in the tools with which they were laid to rest. As the example of Radley suggests, inclusion in these later burials remained a prerogative of both women and men, although the latter tend to occur in greater numbers. Seen by those who attended the rite, the body and its associations spoke of genealogies and affiliations that were sharply defined. Ancestral rites remained pivotal to social life. There were still many ways of dying and many uses to which human remains could be put but, increasingly, the ancestors were drawn upon as instruments for competition and the creation of authority. Instead of standing for and protecting the collective, the dead were recruited as specific lines pursued particular interests. As one generation gave way to another, people reworked the forms and associations of tombs. In this way, they redefined their bonds of kinship and their ties with others.

So far this discussion has remained at a relatively general level. I have asked what it meant to inhabit a patchwork landscape; to move across its surface, and to cut into the earth for stone. I have also begun to explore the places and times that pits and tombs may have occupied. These varied rhythms are important for understanding the place of other sites that we often class as ceremonial – cursus monuments and causewayed enclosures. They sketch in something of the conditions under which these places were encountered. Herding, long fallow cultivation, stone procurement and woodland management did not determine the character of those encounters nor the purposes that they served. However, they were caught up in the reproduction of relations between communities, and perhaps the basic concept of community itself. Not only that, they raised concerns that were often addressed where different groups came together: fertility and renewal; access and ancestry; kinship and obligation; conflict and competition.

Patterns in the characteristics of these sites and activities raise broader questions. The significance of pits or tombs may have been best appreciated at a local scale, and most keenly felt by a small number of people. Yet like pottery and stone tools, these features were created with reference to ideas that stretched a considerable distance across the country and through time. Just as ground and polished axes can be found from northern Scotland to Cornwall, or similarities in core working traced between Yorkshire and Wiltshire, so some of the conventions surrounding the creation of pits or the veneration of ancestors appear to be shared between regions. In other

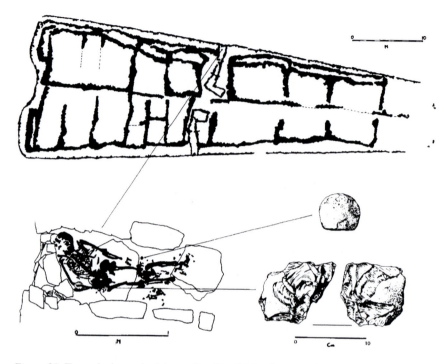

Figure 25 Towards the end of the earlier Neolithic, the articulated body of a man was placed in the entrance to the north chamber of Hazelton long cairn in Gloucestershire. The chamber itself contained the disarticulated remains of several individuals who had been deposited some time before this final act of burial. Close to his hands were a flint core and a pebble hammerstone.

words, we can see common themes and concerns, even though these may have been drawn upon in different ways from one setting to another. These patterns may be partly a product of our own preconceptions, and our desire to find an order that we can call 'national', but they do seem to highlight what at first glance appears to be a paradox. How do we reconcile similarities at these broader scales with the idea that the landscape was dispersed, fragmented and often seasonal in its roll-call? We might make reference to routine mobility patterns or to concepts of exogamy and overlapping local traditions. We may even try to dismiss these trends as no more than a product of time depth, but this fails to capture the character of relations that went beyond horizons of kinship and close affiliation. How was this order possible at all?

8   Attending to the dead

It had been two years since her death. Two years since they had built the frame on which her body was carried to the tomb. A day's walk and a season from the hearth that fed her in her last days. Hazel poles had been cut near the river, fashioned and lashed together by her brothers. Her husband gave food for the funeral. It lasted three nights. On the last, according to custom, she was placed on the threshold, at the entrance to the house of the old ones.

She was between worlds. A quilt of stones was placed across her body to encourage her to stay and, once this was done, there was the handing on of all she had possessed. Her clothes passed to the shoulders of her sister; her tools and skills to the hands of her daughters. Respect was paid and honour done. The line remained. Her name was a part of theirs and it would not be forgotten. When they married, her daughters would carry that name into other lines. When they sat or worked with the other women, she would be remembered.

It was not an easy passing. The winter had crept into her body and no fire could warm her. Her flesh was birch with a thin film of ice. When spring brought a thaw to the hills, she remained cold; her pallor a sign that she had already entered the ghost world. What food they had would not sustain her and though the fire was kept high, death came as she slept. She had seen over thirty summers. That was how it was. No one was sure what had taken such a hold. There were no wounds, no signs. It was simply her time. From then until her funeral, her shade stood by the river, waiting for her kin to arrive from upstream. The shaman had spoken to her but she did not reply. That was often the way. Afterwards, she had been close but difficult to see, her spirit held by the stone on her flesh.

Now it was time for her ghost to leave the company of close kin. The gardens had been thin since her death and her husband's new wife had lost a child at birth. No one was sure. Such events were common enough, often a signal that it was time to move. But there were whispers that it was her, that she was anxious for the company of the old ones and jealous of all she saw but could not touch. It was early, but all agreed that the time had come. It was time to raise her body, to clean her bones and place them with the others.

Preparations took many days. News went upstream, an invitation to attend and honour the dead; it went across the hill, the offer of a chance to bury recent enmities. With luck, the celebrations would sweeten bad blood. Word was returned and the next full moon agreed.

Passed along the line, the word took on a life of its own. It turned in talk around distant hearths and passed along trails through chance encounters. With each new step, it lost a little of its weight and form. Carried downstream, it reached the coast as hearsay, a story of relative strangers, before sinking in the tide of other news.

Her family arrived first. Climbing for a day, they had traced the high stream to its source, then turned west to cross the new pasture. Standing almost to the height of the last few birch stumps, the grass was strong. It would fatten the cattle when the leaves turned brown and they would face the winter with thick flesh on their bones. Talk of who would return with the herd had carried them along. Soon after that, they caught sight of the tomb. Hidden since the start of the climb, it grew on the skyline with each step forward, rising out of the ground to meet them. At one end, the mound of stone and turf tapered down into the hill. At the other, timbers and stone uprights marked the entrance to the house of the dead. Behind the facade were the chambers in which they lay. Camp was made close by, where the open ground came down to meet the forest.

It was right that they were first. Many would come and that meant many mouths to feed. It took time to prepare the ground, to restore and set the hearths. There was also food to be readied, meat to fill the belly and drink to turn the head. Windfalls needed bundling for the fires that would burn while the moon was strong. For two days, men, women and children were scattered across different tasks. On the third, others came along different tracks, adding to the piles of food and fuel. Among kin on such occasions, these were gifts that needed little counter.

By the fourth day, all had gathered. There was food and drink in great abundance and near fifty mouths to make light work of it. Roasting pits were lit and animals slaughtered; the clearing was alive with talk and activity. Work began around the tomb, the different families labouring side by side. They cut back the scrub and restored the flanking ditches, clearing the ground in readiness for the ceremony. Upcast from the ditches was pitched onto the mound, fresh stone, fresh earth, old shards of pottery and bone. With the turn of each year, the mound gained a little more height; the ditches a little more depth.

By late afternoon on the fifth day, activities began to resolve themselves around the tomb. The shaman had arrived and was anxious to begin. The older men from each family removed the blocking from the entrance. A lattice of poles, woven while still green, was cut from the uprights. Two years before, it had been the bier on which the body had been carried from the river. Sun-dried and brittle from the heat of the summer, the poles cracked and split as they were pulled from the frame. These would be tinder for the fire that burnt the last of her flesh. That done, the stones were lifted from the body by the women who had shared her hearth. Others squatted along the edge of the shadow cast by the mound.

The seasons had been kind. Much of the body she had worn in life was already gone and that which remained fell easily from her frame. Her sister collected these last remnants. She gathered the hair and flesh in a simple clay vessel and as she worked, she took care to pick the smaller bones from the earth, the fingers that had once pressed clay and gripped stone, the teeth worn from years of chewing leather. Only a few had been carried away. The larger bones were brought out from the shadows, turned and stacked in the forecourt for all to see. Some talked about the woman they remembered and of the times when they had come to this place in her company. Others talked of absent kin and of the winter that lay ahead, breaking off to kick at the dogs when they strayed too close to the pile. Conversation drifted and turned while the sun sank below the horizon and it was then that the shaman and the elders stepped forward.

Bones before him and open tomb behind, the shaman faced the living. All but the youngest knew the pattern of what would follow. He began with the invocation of names, the chain of generations that tied present to past. As he talked, he mapped the tale across the land that stretched away in front of them. He held it in his hands. Stood alongside, the elders nodded or muttered in agreement when invited by a pause between the words. Some listened intently, embroidering the tale with comments whispered to those nearby. Others turned their attention to the fires and to other tasks.

Spoken in full, the litany of names charted the histories of families who cut back and forth across each others' paths. Yet it was more than the line or even the clan. The tale knew few boundaries. It dwelt on recent years and it travelled outside time and the circle of seasons. Those who listened heard of the first people born from river and forest and of the forms and places each clan had taken. When the old ones died, they turned again to the forms they had assumed in life or sank into the land itself. Yet even now, they looked after the line, keeping them on good paths and sometimes entering the dreams that came with initiation. They held the land and the people together. Those who came after built tombs in their honour, raising stone and earth to hold their essence.

As he talked, the shaman tipped the contents of a small bag into his hand. Knuckles of flint and blood-red pebbles, a yellow boar's tusk and a snail made of stone. All rattled together as he turned them in his palm. He selected a small cone of flint as a prop to his telling. The darkness of the stone was obscured by a patina like cataracts across old eyes, but the ridges and scars could still be seen. They ran in parallel from head to foot, straight and true round the body. This was a core from the old times. There were few left who could work this way. Closing his fingers around the stone, he brought the old ones into the clearing.

As the shadows deepened, he turned and ducked into the tomb. Once inside, his voice became muffled and difficult to follow. The stone held his words. Those outside drew closer, came into the shadow. With two of the elders, the shaman held a light to the bones in each chamber, some stacked, some scattered in apparent disarray. Fragments became animated as the flickering torch came close. Turning broken orbits in his hands, he called on those who were present by name. He spoke directly and did not lose his way. He told them of the woman who had rested at their door for the past two years, of her family and her place in the line. He called on them to welcome her to the company of the ancestors so that she too could watch over her kin. Like the tomb, her vigilance would last for all time.

Two of the older women took his words as their cue. Moving forward, they picked up the skull and the longer bones and carried them into the tomb, stooping as they passed beneath the lintel. Once inside, they placed them in the chamber in the company of those long dead. They took care to see that the skull faced out of the chamber and towards the world beyond. Their task complete, they peered beyond the shaman to where the old ones lay before stepping back outside.

By now the moon had risen, and beneath the pale disc even the living looked like ghosts. Faces close at hand were lit by the fire that burned beneath flesh and hair and, once these had flown, more wood was added. Gradually, the flames pushed the darkness back towards the edge of the clearing. Other hearths were lit and food was brought forward. Songs and dances followed soon after and, as the evening wore on, the bones that remained outside the tomb were handed out among the line. Some would be buried at the place of her birth, to rest near the hearth that first gave her strength. Others would be kept in the rafters of scattered houses to hold her watchful presence. A few would be saved for the next gathering. There they would join with others in the circle of the clan.

Sat by the brightest hearths, the elders nodded as they talked. Pots that carried food to their fire were drained then dashed against the stones of the facade. Shards scattered beyond the light to be trampled underfoot or scuffed into ditches.

This was how things should be done, things in order and in their right time. There had been too many deaths among the children. New blood and seed corn had been lost. Those so young they had not met the dead were returned to the river. There was nothing to fix them to the line, no point on which they could hold fast. The return to the river meant a chance to be born again. Here at least the path had been true. There were no parents to mourn the passing of their children and the death had brought many together. There was still much talking to be done; concessions to be made and blood fines to be settled, but the signs were good. The families were once again sharing food and fire. There would be calm for some time after people had scattered.

Rybury.

Haddenham.

Figure 26

9 A time and a place for enclosure

Up on the edge of the Vale of Pewsey a chalk ridge hangs above the arable, an area of grazing and hawthorn scrub. We know it now as Knap Hill. Coming to this vantage in the low light of morning or as the sun starts to set, the shadows reveal a chain of ephemeral features, shallow depressions and low banks follow the contours of the hill, marking the line of a large, intermittent enclosure cut into the chalk. Viewed from the crest, this circuit seems to lie on the threshold between two lands. There is the vale below, open now and cultivated to the horizon. There are the higher reaches of the hills, land held in common only a few centuries ago. Between the two run folds in the chalk, broad grooves across the contour that are both watersheds and paths of least resistance.

Many have recruited this threshold. Bronze Age barrows lie scattered across the rise, seen as people passed with stock. A Roman signal station also made use of the ridge, a place of observation and a reminder to others of the order of things. The silted ditches of feudal land divisions follow the same changes in the chalk, forgotten boundaries now bisected by the road. There are older features too, features that would have been familiar to earlier Neolithic communities. On the crest of an adjacent rise lies the barrow known as Adam's Grave. A reference to the origin myths of a more recent past, its older names are no longer held in social memory. The mound lies swathed in turf pulled up from surrounding pasture. Like the enclosure, it seems a part of the land rather than an imposition.

It was not always this way. Scatters of flint, like the earthworks themselves, hint at different social geographies. The periodic ploughing of pasture throws up worked stone consistent with earlier Neolithic traditions. Narrow flakes and blades are common, as are the cores from which they were struck. There are also tools and waste which suggest the presence of people on this rise during the later Mesolithic, smaller, carefully worked cores and a few fine microliths. Discarded and deposited over many generations, these scatters reflect varied roll-calls. They are the camps of a few and the gatherings of many; close kin gathered round a hearth and larger companies assembled on or near the crest. There are also hints of a diversity of activities: the clearing of ground and the cutting of chalk; the herding of cattle and the working of

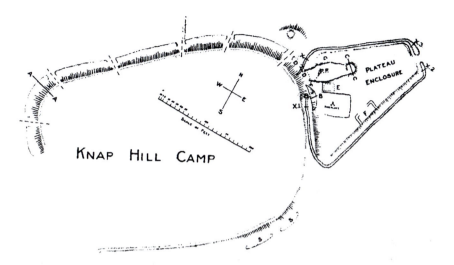

Figure 27 Knap Hill, Wiltshire. 'It is impracticable to regard these breaks in the entrenchment as due to an unfinished undertaking, or as entrances in any ordinary sense, and the only other feasible theory seems to be that they had some distinct purpose in the scheme of defence; that they were, indeed, a strengthening and not a weakening factor in this seemingly not very strongly defended place' (Cunnington 1912: 48).

stone; encounters with others and perhaps with ancestors. Varied tasks, varied people, various times; scales of action that broke with day-to-day experience.

In chapter 7, I concluded by asking how the dispersed social conditons of the earlier Neolithic could give rise to widespread similarities in material traditions. In one sense at least, the question is easily answered. In many small-scale societies, it is common for limited communities to recognise themselves as elements within extensive networks, webs of relations that they continually acknowledge and renew. These more extensive ties can be addressed through the exchange of artefacts or through the acquisition of more intangible resources such as esoteric knowledge. Often, there is a tangible fascination for the distant, brought into focus where marriage links different lines of descent and in the negotiation of political authority at a local scale. Quotidian life also involves contact with others and an acknowledgement of ties that go beyond the everyday horizon. This was also true of the earlier Neolithic. What remains to be asked is how the larger monuments of the time, including enclosures such as Knap Hill, contributed to the playing out of this process. What can we say about the histories of these monuments? Where were they in the broader landscapes of the time?

Figure 28 Knap Hill from the ground.

Recent histories

Knap Hill is by no means the largest or the most celebrated of earlier Neolithic enclosures. Unlike Windmill Hill, it did not become a type site for culture historians. Nor has it been the subject of recent excavations like those at Crickley Hill or Hambledon. Its name appears most frequently in inventories. Yet for all of this uncertainty, Knap Hill is important because it shares a number of characteristics with these places, features that have come to be regarded as classic or typical. There is its elevated position high on the chalk: the enclosure looks down upon the surrounding land and, from the south at least, the hill can be traced on the skyline more than a day's walk away. There are the ditches and causeways themselves, dips in the turf which hold the last snow. Occurring as single or multiple circuits and sometimes incomplete, these features are often irregular, intermittent and variable in their scale.

Enclosures with these signatures were some of the first to be recorded in the modern era, most commonly in Wessex and Sussex. Since then, radiocarbon dating has shown that they began to be built not long after the first tombs, perhaps as early as 3800 BC, a tradition that was worked and reworked for as much as thirty generations. A few were originally confirmed through work on the Iron Age hill-forts imposed on the same high points. All could be recognised at the time because of the place that they had occupied in the later, historic landscape. Most were set above intensive intakes and favoured for grazing as much as for arable, sites like Whitesheet Hill, Rybury or Barkhale. Many had been features in common land or on the upper edges of wood pasture, passed on a seasonal basis by people moving stock or travelling between villages. Some were occupied in other ways; medieval and post-medieval cultivation ridges and related features can be traced within the boundaries of several sites. Others were passed or ploughed unnoticed and, in general, the imprint of ownership and production has not bitten so deep as it has on lower ground. Protected now as scheduled monuments, these earthworks have taken on a new significance. Prominent in landscapes of heritage and in nostalgic depictions of the countryside, they are familiar landmarks in our accounts.

Enclosures have been classified as members of a distinct archaeological category since the early part of this century, particularly since the 1920s. At that time, scholars such as Curwen, Kendrick and Hawkes drew attention to the character of the ditches on these sites, seeing in their form a definitive trait. The broken, segmented character of their boundaries was the inspiration for many of the terms that have been used since then for description and definition: causewayed camp; interrupted ditch enclosure; causewayed enclosure. Since their time, fieldwork has added to the list of traits that appear to 'go with' enclosures. Where survival is good, excavations often reveal deposits of animal bone, burials and fragmentary human remains. Much is also made of pottery or stone axes made from non-local materials on a number of sites.

The search for similarities is a hallmark of a good deal of archaeological research. Yet there are times when our categories turn back upon the evidence, when similarities obscure important differences from one site or region to another. In the case of enclosures, patterns of similarity have led many to conclude that one site was much like another, that they were used and understood in similar ways. These arguments have proved persuasive. There are parallels between sites and they do seem to reflect the recognition of common ideas and the playing out of familiar themes. Yet, like tombs, it is clear that these ideas were drawn upon rather differently from one time and place to another. Excavation has revealed important differences in character and content. Certain features may be shared, but individual enclosures have varied histories. Some appear to have been quite short-lived, used in various ways for no more than a few generations. Others have histories that span several centuries, sites like Hembury and Abingdon. There are also differences of scale and form. Enclosures like Crickley Hill and Maiden Castle encompass several hectares. Whitesheet Hill and Rybury have ditches that remain visible on the surface. Others can seem quite diminutive in comparison, with narrow, shallow ditches less than a metre wide and circuits that enclose less than half a hectare.

Differences can also be seen in the number and character of circuits, so much so that it is best to talk simply of enclosures. Some, like Langford and Coombe Hill, are discontinuous but many, like Etton, take the form of a single ditch, often with an internal bank. Others, like Sawbridgeworth and Briar Hill, have two, three or four concentric circuits; at Whitehawk in Sussex there may even be five. Excavation suggests that this was often a product of change over time. At Windmill Hill and others it seems that circuits were added to the original enclosure, increasing the complexity and depth of the monuments. At Fornham All Saints, a pair of enclosures suggest succession and replacement close at hand and this may also be true of the more distanced 'pair' of sites at Knap Hill and Rybury. If this was not enough, there are other differences in the ways that these circuits were developed or changed over time. Some enclosures began life as circuits of pits. Many also have multiple causeways which remained in use throughout their development. Some, like Carn Brea and Helman Tor in Cornwall, and Carrock Fell in Cumbria, have stone circuits that incorporate or enclose prominent outcrops and earthfast boulders. In addition, there are a number where old causeways were eventually removed in favour of more continuous ditches and palisades, sites like Haddenham in the Cambridgeshire Fens. Common themes but uncommon histories.

Aerial photography over the past two decades has also transformed our understanding of frequency and distribution. Contrary to traditional wisdom, enclosures are not confined to a few chalk hills. They may be more visible on hills and promontories, and this may be why they dominate early syntheses.

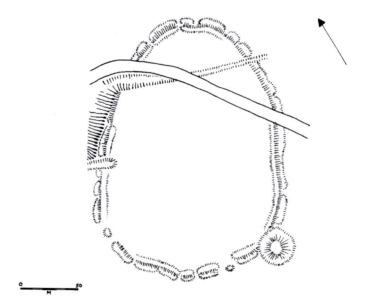

Figure 29 Whitesheet Hill, Wiltshire (after Piggott 1952). Drawing attention to the lack of evidence for permanent settlement in many excavated enclosures, Stuart Piggott stressed their role as cattle kraals and as seasonal rallying points for scattered pastoral groups.

But they are more than matched by similar sites in other settings, revealed in the crops and parched soils of summer, or exposed where alluvium is stripped from gravel. Enclosures occur on lower ground; on river terraces and on the slopes of broad lowland valleys, places like Briar Hill, Uffington and Freston. A few, like Abingdon, even have rivers as parts of their boundaries.

New sites have also appeared beyond the margins of standard distributions, along the Thames Valley, in the Midlands and on the edges of the Fens, valleys like the Nene and the Welland. There are also examples in Cumbria, Wales, Yorkshire, Northumberland and perhaps even in Scotland. New names are continually being added to the list: Barholm, Broadwell, Buckland and Down Ampney, Alrewas, Icomb and Maiden Bower. These more extensive distributions have encouraged the search for regional traditions. Using scale and the frequency and spacing of ditch circuits, some have suggested that lines can be drawn between areas like the Thames Valley and Wessex, or between the West Midlands and the East. These arguments have their attractions, but the suggested regions are actually rather blurred. They overlap, just as relations between different social networks would have overlapped at the time, and there are more localised patterns. Similarities in the form of sites within a region can suggest more focussed traditions, places like Etton, Uffington, Barholm and Northborough around the Fen Edge; Bury Hill, Court Hill and Halnaker Hill on the South Downs.

How have these sites been interpreted? One of the more persistent responses has been to regard enclosures as settlements that were more or less permanently occupied. Early accounts drew parallels with Iron Age hill-forts, particularly where these later earthworks were found on the same ridges and crests. Cut through with references to Homer and the Bible, and emphasising the elevated position of known sites, accounts stressed their value as defended settlements. This was a prominent feature in Maud Cunnington's discussion of Knap Hill, where multiple causeways offered the chance of counter-attack when inhabitants were beseiged. Such arguments made sense at the time, and the classical sources appeared to provide numerous parallels. Land and stock might be objects of competition and this prompted a need for the sorts of protection that these earliest 'hill-forts' seemed to offer. It was as if the traditional model of a warlike, tribal Iron Age could be stretched back and imposed upon these traces of earlier times.

Looked at more closely and with the benefit of hindsight, these arguments have been difficult to sustain, just as they are for many later hill-forts themselves. A few enclosures bear the scars of conflict and violent death, sites such as Carn Brea, Crickley Hill and Hambledon. In each case, however, these events came only at the end of long and varied histories. There are many sites where the banks and ditches were either so diminutive, variable or interrupted that they would have been of little practical use. As Francis Pryor observed at Etton, enclosures may encompass specific areas, but they often do so with 'manifest and calculated inefficiency'. Others do not make a complete circuit, sites like Cardington and Hampton Lucy, or are located in ways that

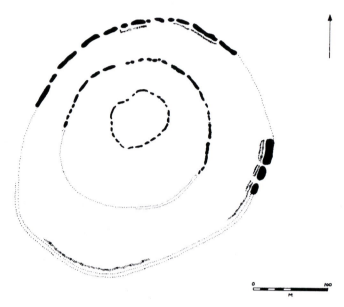

Figure 30 Windmill Hill, Wiltshire. Where many had talked of the place of
        enclosures in a pastoral economy, Isobel Smith was one of the first to tackle
        the social dimensions of their use. Emphasising the common pattern of
        deliberate backfilling and the structured contents of ditches, Smith inferred
        periodic use for a variety of communal ceremonial events. '. . . the
        inescapable conclusion seems to be that the causewayed enclosures were
        not meant to be permanent enclosures at all, and that their function was a
        non-utilitarian one' (Smith 1966: 474).

make little practical sense were defence a paramount concern. If they served
that role at all, they did so in symbolic terms. Some are clearly elevated or on
promontories, as at Peak Camp and Dorstone Hill. Others, like Windmill
Hill, extended down across the shoulder of hillsides. They could be looked
into from above and their interiors were often framed by bank and ditch for
observers looking up from valleys and clearings below. Often the viewsheds
of these places were partial and focussed, as if they were meant to be seen by
those who lived or travelled across particular lands and in particular directions.
    A similar setting can be seen close to Long Meg and her Daughters in
Cumbria. Here the uprights on one edge of the stone circle appear to lie in or
next to the ditch of a much larger enclosure. Both are cut by the ridges and
headlands of medieval cultivation. Now only visible from the air, this earlier
monument avoids the immediate crest. Even at Knap Hill, which is discontinuous and sits on the apex of a prominent chalk ridge, the use of the
topography is difficult to understand in strategic terms alone. The earthworks
are most prominent on the north side where the ground rolls down to a wide,
natural bowl in the chalk. To the south the slope is both steeper and longer,

perhaps providing a sufficient sense of demarcation in itself. However, the ground rises sharply inside the enclosure, highlighting the arrangement and activity of those contained within its bounds. Here and elsewhere it is as if the immediate topography was exploited to make the most of this potential.

Variations on this theme can also be seen at Gardom's Edge in the Peak District, where an interrupted bank cuts off a prominent stretch of gritstone cliff. Like Carn Brea and Carrock Fell, the boundary of this enclosure is built of stone. Looking west, the view is impressive. The ground falls away at your feet and it is possible to gaze across the Derwent Valley and towards more distant hills. Those who stood here in the earlier Neolithic would have looked down upon a heavily wooded landscape, at clearings and at trails that stretched into the distance. They would have seen the smoke of different communities or people moving cattle near the river. From below, the cliff marks the location of the enclosure, the site being one of a number where a dramatic scarp or edge was recruited to form part of the boundary. For those passing through the valley, the cliff would have been a point of reference, a dominant feature on the skyline and perhaps in local memory. Looking east,

Figure 31 Aerial photograph of Long Meg and her Daughters (Cumbria), showing the outline of a larger (and probably earlier) enclosure which appears to underlie one side of the later stone circle. (Photo: Bob Bewley. Crown copyright reserved.)

the view is rather different. The ground behind the cliff dips slightly, so that the enclosure seems elevated when close at hand. It then rises towards Birchen Edge and a vantage into the enclosure is easily obtained. Variable in form and constuction, the making of the bank involved the accumulation and piling of gritstone boulders. At certain points along its course, larger stones can still be seen which indicate the presence of a rudimentary facade. Yet, despite these features, it is difficult to conceive of the monument as a practical barrier. Stone has been robbed for use in the medieval sheepfold and later estate boundaries that lie close at hand. The bank was also cut by tracks that took millstones from quarries on the edge, but it would never have been particularly high, and certainly not a barrier to vision when approached from the east. This was also the case in more lowland settings at places like Briar Hill and Etton.

There were, of course, exceptions to this rule. There were times when vision into the interior would have been impeded for those near many sites. Where banks and other structures rose to more than two metres in height or made use of the immediate topography, both vision and movement were directly constrained. Nowhere was this potential realised so dramatically as at Crickley Hill and Hambledon, where substantial palisades were constructed towards the end of the time that the enclosures were in use. These would have been striking features, but they cannot be taken as typical. At other enclosures, the ditches were often slight and banks modest and variable if they were raised at all. Many boundaries were actually rather permeable; if movement was constrained, it was by custom and convention.

What of the more basic assumption that the majority of enclosures were constructed as settlements? This has proved to be a resilient theme. A common feature of many accounts has been the idea that enclosures were somehow central to social and economic life for earlier Neolithic groups. As places of occupation, they were the pivots around which activities turned. Windmill Hill even became the type site and the axis for a specific 'culture'. Often there is a sense of an enclosure lying at the centre of a broader catchment, of people passing in and out in the course of daily life. During the first few decades of

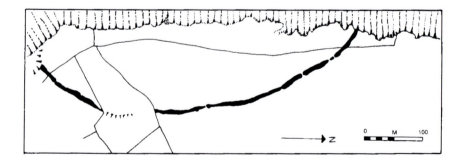

Figure 32 The stone-banked enclosure at Gardom's Edge, Derbyshire.

this century the ditches themselves were regarded as the focus of domestic activity. Noting the presence of stone, pottery, bone and ash in many features, Cecil Curwen suggested that these were the subterranean homes of 'pit-dwellers'. For him and for others at the time, the evidence suggested a squalid existence, lives eked out amid detritus and decay. The recovery of human bones from these ditches only served to confirm the base nature of settlement at the time. People seemed content to live cheek by jowl with their dead, the fragmentary character of the remains hinting at a lack of respect and perhaps even cannibalism.

By the middle of the century these arguments had been refuted by excavation, analogy and closer study. However, settlement itself remained as a common theme, enclosures cast as the residences of early farmers or pastoral groups. More recently, settlement hierarchies have been constructed with enclosures placed near the top of the ladder. Some have been cast as elite residences, places from which those with a measure of regional authority held sway over others. Not surprisingly, these arguments have been made most forcefully where the sites in question command elevated positions.

It may be unwise to assume that political geographies in the earlier Neolithic were necessarily a constant from one region or even one generation to another. In any case, our evidence is impossibe to reconcile with these singular interpretations. Where excavated, a number of enclosures show signs of occupation, but the evidence is not that easy to read. Some, like Carn Brea and perhaps other south-western sites, do seem to have been a focus for settlement. There may have been times when larger numbers gathered at these places, yet they also had a close association with specific groups who lived and laboured in their immediate environs. The same may be true for sites such as Staines and Crickley Hill, but in each case it is unclear whether occupation was permanent throughout the life history of the site. Residence may have been a feature of only certain phases of use. A changing association with settlement can also be seen at Abingdon and Hambledon Hill. Both saw a lengthy phase of periodic activity before occupation became a commonplace. At Hambledon, this was concentrated in a small enclosure on a distinct chalk spur. By contrast, episodes of settlement may have preceded the creation of the first enclosure at Windmill Hill and at Robin Hood's Ball.

Internal features do not make our task any easier. We simply do not know what lies within the boundaries of many sites, and even when we do our evidence is not straightforward. Some contain the traces of varied buildings, stake alignments and so on, but their phasing remains problematic and, again, they are not ubiquitous. Pits on the other hand, are found within the boundaries of many sites. Often their contents have a formal or structured character that recalls the patterns seen in features beneath scatters. We might easily take these as signs of occupation and, in certain cases, this is probably wise. However, the idea of settlement over many generations is difficult to sustain where there is little or no evidence for dense palimpsests of related features. Here again it seems better to conclude that there was no singular pattern to the ways these monuments were inhabited. If anything, periodic use was probably more common than permanent settlement.

This brings us to a curious feature of the ditches that define many sites. Like pits, these can also contain quite structured deposits, so much so that they can seem like larger variations on the same theme. Close inspection of ditch sections reveals that many did not lie open for all that long. The ditches at Briar Hill were dug, backfilled and re-dug on a number of occasions, and this pattern was repeated at places like Maiden Castle and Etton. These patterns can sometimes be explained as a product of the slumping of banks or the clearing of silts which were dumped on the outer edge of a ditch. However, it is not always so straightforward. Backfilling can appear quite deliberate and recutting relatively formal. In effect, the boundaries of a number of sites were taken in and out of commission. This was not simply the result of some routine process of ditch cleaning and maintenance: it was a product of more purposeful acts that pulled individual enclosures in and out of focus. Once again, this is difficult to square with permanent occupation. Not only that, it raises the possibility that these monuments were regarded differently from one year or generation to another. Like the broader landscape itself, it seems that the character and the roll-call of events at many enclosures was actually quite varied.

What of the immediate environs of these sites? What was going on beyond

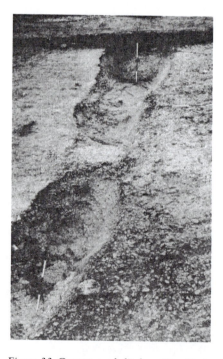

Figure 33 Causewayed ditch at Hambledon Hill. (Photo courtesy of Roger Mercer.)

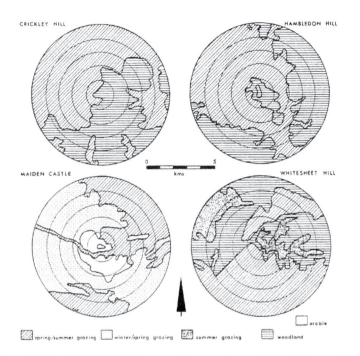

Figure 34 Land-use potentials around four enclosures (after Barker and Webley 1978).

their ditches and banks? Reading some accounts, the mind's eye conjures a picture of open country, of an ordered landscape in which the routines of mixed farming radiated out from a settled core. This image has been powerful and has been reinforced by many reconstruction drawings. It has led some to assess the productive potential of the land and resources around particular sites as an index of their sustainability. Here again, the situation is not that simple. Such a model does no justice to broader routines of movement and activity at the time, and it is not really echoed in our evidence. Some enclosures were close to upland pasture, lush grasses to fatten stock before the bite of winter. Others were closer to low-lying water meadows or to woodlands where pigs foraged on the margins of clearings. They occupied different places in the seasonal round.

What of signs of settlement itself? Scatters that are broadly contemporary are sometimes found in the environs of enclosures. We can see this at Knap Hill, Kedington and Robin Hood's Ball. However, this is not always the case – there can be a distance. Contemporary scatters can lie a day's walk away and enclosures can seem almost physically marginal. Even when material is present, it may not reflect settlement inhabited throughout the time that particular enclosures remained in use. Palimpsests and small scatters of worked stone may just as easily reflect episodic activity, camps and larger collectives gathered for limited periods. Support for this idea can be found in the snail shells and relict pollen from a number of sites. Where evidence survives, we find a picture which blurs our otherwise neat image. The land around some was already open when the first ditch was dug. Others were established in limited woodland clearings and this remained their milieu throughout the times of their use. Whatever the extent to which vision was impaired by bank or palisade, some at least would have been difficult to see even when relatively close at hand. The cutting of the ditches involved the clearance of timber and the extension of open ground, firing and felling the first stages in the process of construction. For communities used to small clearings, this may have seemed a familiar arrangement. The presence of woodlands and the evidence of clearance struck a well-known chord; it was how much of life was ordered and experienced. But like the broader patchwork these circumstances were far from static. The environs of enclosures were reworked over time; opened, regenerated, inhabited and abandoned. They saw a diversity of occupation – pauses for days, gatherings for weeks, perhaps even residence for a handful of years. The pattern of encounters varied from site to site and from one year or season to the next. In the fragmented landscapes of the time, the way people used these places was not a given.

This is not an original idea. Present in accounts over the past few decades has been the suggestion that many enclosures were used in the more episodic or 'event-like' fashion suggested by certain ditch sections. Some have argued that they served as cattle kraals, sites of seasonal occupation for pastoral communities and their animals. This has recently been suggested for a large, more continuous enclosure with opposed entrances at Coupland in Northumberland. Seen in this light, boundaries reflect the need to contain important stock, with limited occupation in the interior or nearby. These arguments have their attractions. The husbandry of stock was bound up in the use of many enclosures and, where it survives, cattle bone is a common element. At sites like Staines some of the accumulated bone may be a product of phases of occupation. At Hambledon Hill the structure of the cattle bone assemblage suggests husbandry for dairying. Yet there is more to it than that. Not all enclosures have these associations. Evidence for occupation is variable and the complexity of boundaries on many sites makes little sense in stock management terms alone. Use for stock is also difficult to argue for scarp edge sites, or those where the immediate environs remained heavily wooded. The link with cattle is certainly a strong one, but we cannot assume that the practical requirements of stock husbandry dictated either the form or the character of events at these places. In any case, such arguments can make little sense of the more formal deposits found on many sites. Amongst other things, cattle bones are often found as components in deposits in ditches and pits, articulated meaty joints or bundles of limbs placed in the earth in a structured and deliberate manner.

What often gets missed is the sense of variety and change in the encounter that people had with these places. Visited periodically, many enclosures were points along the pathways that people trod with their animals. Founded on ecotones, sites like Knap Hill and Rybury sat on the threshold that separated seasons. They were between the lands of winter and summer and, even in more lowland settings, they were often marginal to the places in which people lived for much of the time. This was not a constant, but it is important if we want to grasp how these sites were often understood. Where these monuments were set apart, they could be regarded as places and times which departed from the world of the everyday.

How the use of enclosures was tied to the seasonal round is difficult to determine. It is unlikely that all saw a consistent pattern of gathering and/or occupation every year. Present on a number of sites, hazelnut shells and the bones of young animals suggest an association with late summer and autumn for some events at least. A cache of cleaned grain recovered at Hambledon Hill might indicate a similar season. In each case, however, we have to allow that these resources can be stored. At Etton the situation is a little clearer. The site was effectively waterlogged and perhaps even flooded at certain times of the year and the same may be true for other low-lying sites such as Cardington and Broadwell. The question of seasonality remains open, but it cannot be dismissed. Events at enclosures were embedded in the broader routines that people followed and, under these conditions, tradition may have dictated the appropriate times of year in which a gathering might take place. No doubt there were also times when tides in the affairs of particular kin-groups required a gathering that cut across the customary seasons. The roll-call of these events could be brief indeed – a camp for a few days and a visit by members of a particular family – but these monuments also saw the fires of many hearths, a mixing of people with varied lineages and different interests. It is this sense of variety that we find in Isobel Smith's characterisation of Windmill Hill as a 'rallying point' for a dispersed population.

Continental drift

What purposes were served by these varied events? What did it mean to come with close kin, to gather with others or even to live for a time within the bounds of these sites? There can be no simple answer. Enclosures were not built for a single purpose and they did not develop in a singular manner. Much the same situation can be traced on the continent, the source from which this idea of 'altering the earth' was ultimately derived. Some forty years ago, Stuart Piggott drew close parallels between a number of continental enclosures and sites in Britain. For him and for many since, these shared traits implied contact, communication and perhaps even colonisation. It is now more common to discuss these trends in terms of the movement of ideas rather than the migration of people, but the parallels are there nonetheless, evidence that these ideas were drawn upon in a variety of ways.

Circuits of interrupted ditches have been identified in several countries: the Netherlands, Belgium, Germany, France and southern Scandinavia. There are even enclosures in central Europe which reflect the recognition of similar themes. More often than not, identification has progressed as it has in Britain, from upland earthworks to more low-lying crop-marks. Yet in any one region, there are variations in forms, locations and histories, confirmation that superficial resemblances can be misleading. Chronology varies considerably as does the character and content of different sites. Some of the earliest enclosures predate those in Britain by more than a millennium. Dating to the centuries around 5000 BC they are associated with some of the latest settlements of the *Linearbandkeramik* (LBK), an archaeologically defined cultural tradition spanning much of central and parts of western Europe. Characteristic features of the LBK include post-built longhouses, the use of domesticates and the pottery which gives the tradition its name.

Conventionally, the LBK is often explained as the product of a process of colonisation from the south-east, the vanguard of a 'wave of advance' that brought intrusive populations into contact and even conflict with indigenous gatherers and hunters. How far this tradition can be treated as uniform remains a subject of much debate, as does the idea that all aspects of settlement and material culture reflect a process of colonisation. Recent accounts have emphasised a view of these developments as a product of changes in local conditions, playing down the scale and impact of an inexorable colonial process. There is still much that we cannot articulate about these patterns. Here it is enough to note that in parts of what are now Belgium, Germany

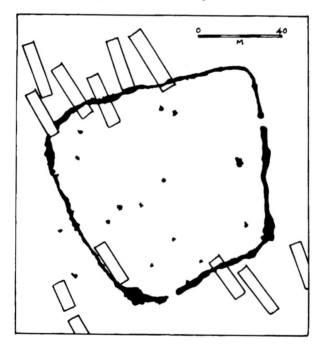

Figure 35 The relationship between the enclosure and earlier longhouses at Langweiller 8.

and France, distinctive longhouse settlements have been found in association with enclosures with interrupted ditches. These are exceptions to the norm – the majority of LBK settlements have no such associations.

The relationship between LBK longhouses and enclosures is a complex one. As in Britain, there are sites defined by single circuits, places like Darion in Belgium, where an internal palisade ran parallel to a shallow ditch system. Others, such as Langweiler 8, have multiple boundaries and several phases of development. Excavation has also shown that enclosures were generally added towards the end of the time that LBK settlements saw active use, sometimes even postdating them. Some were constructed around longhouses that were still in use. Others were cut around areas containing buildings that had fallen into disrepair, their timbers rotted or removed for use elsewhere. Continuous or discontinuous circuits were also cut between or adjacent to buildings. In these cases, the interiors can seem relatively empty.

Once again, arguments for a defensive role are difficult to sustain in all but a few cases and many sites make little sense as stock pounds. What seems to have been more important was that ditches and associated structures demarcated an area in which certain communal activities could be undertaken. Sometimes it was a space between houses that received this added definition, a place where a community had mingled and performed various tasks for more than a generation. Sometimes it was the site of an old longhouse. In both settings, the cutting of an enclosure drew attention to features that occupied a place in local memory. These could become a focus for other activities. At both Darion and Spiennes, concentrations of waste from stone-working suggest an emphasis upon tool production, the products being taken for use or exchange elsewhere. It is as if certain tasks were singled out, including those that linked a community to the broader social landscape. Other sites suggest an emphasis upon the preparation and consumption of food within a communally defined area, consumption at a level beyond the household.

The cutting of these enclosures created a threshold to be crossed by those undertaking various tasks and a line with which to draw distinctions between people. Just what those distinctions were is difficult to determine on these earliest sites. Some have suggested that the idea of enclosure arose in a climate of increased uncertainty, a response to threats that came from beyond the immediate social group. Even when they were of little practical use, these boundaries emphasised difference through principles of exclusion and inclusion. Perhaps they afforded spiritual protection against others. Perhaps they also contained activities that linked specific communities into more disparate networks of kinship and alliance. Other arguments have stressed the playing out of more local concerns, seeing enclosures as places at which relations within communities were addressed. Where ditches encircled houses, it may be that the line was drawn between different families within the community, the authority of some being marked by their physical separation. It might also be that enclosed houses became the preserve of specific gender groups, or

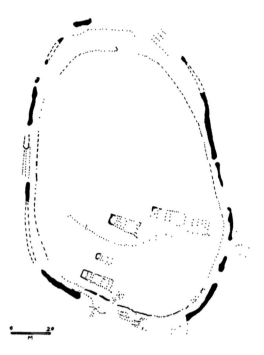

Figure 36 Longhouses and enclosure at Darion, Belgium.

places for local ceremony. Both of these arguments are tempting and they are by no means mutually exclusive. But there is little evidence to develop them and they are of little use where internal structures, pits or ditch deposits are more or less absent.

The situation becomes a little clearer in developments after the LBK. After 5000 BC, the seemingly homogeneous LBK phenomenon, sustained perhaps by regular contact over considerable distances, began to break apart. During the fourth millennium, there was a marked increase in the regionalisation of pottery styles, and in funerary and associated ancestral rites. The changing character of this process is captured in the proliferation of culture names that remain in use on the continent to this day: Rossen then Michelsberg in the Rhinelands, Cerny then Chasseen in northern France and so on. It was against this background of growing regionalisation that the idea of enclosures was again taken up.

The histories of these enclosures are as varied as those traced in the evidence from Britain. Some at least were a focus for settlement, but many contain no traces of occupation. Others seem to have served a defensive role, although this was not contingent on the presence of a resident population. In eastern France, for example, enclosures with substantial stone ramparts presented a dramatic barrier to both vision and movement, but have few signs that they encompassed dwellings. What is common to many is the practice of marking out an area with interrupted ditches and associated structures. As in Britain, some have a single ditch while others have several circuits and even palisades. A number have complex outworks focussed on the principal causeways. Many also have features containing structured or formal deposits, sites like Mairy in the Ardennes and Menneville in the Aisne valley. Placed deposits of animal bone, often joints showing signs of articulation, have been recovered from the ditches and pits on enclosures at Michelsberg and Noyen sur Seine. There are also human remains, fragments of bodies (often skulls) found in similar contexts, and burials, including those of children. Sometimes these bones are found in association with exotic tools or pottery, placed in the earth while still whole.

These themes cohere at Sarup in Denmark. Here there is evidence for two major phases, each with distinct layouts of bank, ditch and palisade that cut off a promontory of land between two rivers. The construction of the two enclosures was separated by a few generations at the most, the first dating to around 2630 BC. Neither of the main phases contains evidence for permanent occupation. Although there are signs that the ditches were backfilled and recut on more than one occasion, both phases were relatively short-lived. It was only after the latest ditches had been backfilled or silted that the area became a focus for open settlement. The substantial ditches and internal pits at Sarup appear to have been the focus for acts of formal deposition in the first phase. These acts involved the interment of human skulls and skull fragments,

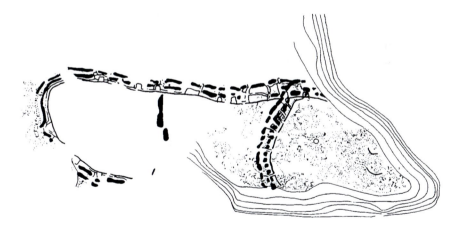

Figure 37 The two phases of enclosure at Sarup, Denmark.

axes, food residues, burnt stone and pottery. The evidence suggests gatherings, feasts and complex rites of passage. The principal entrance to the first enclosure was also a highly elaborate affair and a focus for the deliberate smashing of pottery. Encompassing around three hectares, the second enclosure was just over a third of the size of the first. Yet here again, there was a similar emphasis upon formal deposition in pits and a similar range of deposits. Research also suggests that the treatment of material varied from one part of this later enclosure to another. Artefacts such as axes or pottery are rarely found together in internal features but are associated towards the perimeter of the site in some of the ditches. It seems that subtle conventions guided their deposition in different places and perhaps during different rites.

Enclosures like Sarup and many others on the continent may not make much sense as settlements, but they were a focus for a considerable number of people – the simple fact of their scale implies the labour of many. They reflect the creation of a bounded area in which to undertake important activities: rites of passage, the making of offerings, and the veneration of ancestors. Some were used in this way for a handful of generations, others had longer histories and witnessed changes in character, sometimes becoming places of occupation. In all of these respects, they find echoes in the evidence from Britain. Varied from one place and time to another, events at these sites involved aggregation. They brought different communities together and offered a potential for the negotiation of ties that went beyond immediate blood. In one sense at least, they provided a medium for constructing the idea of society itself.

Constructing society

How were these themes recognised on the ground in Britain? What impact did they have at the level of the communities who passed or gathered at enclosures? Answers to these questions often stress the contents of sites, but we are dealing here with more than containers. These were places that had to be built and attended to. This is a quality of many monuments. Without observance they can be forgotten, becoming 'heritage' to be recruited in other ways. That observance includes the act of building itself.

The process of construction has received some attention. There has been talk of designs, engineering and of broad phases of development, distinct and successive stages in the evolution of monumental forms. It often seems as if the layout of a monument was determined by a blueprint held in the hand of an architect. This tendency finds its clearest expression in estimates of the labour expended in construction. Twenty-five years ago, Colin Renfrew used the effort invested in Neolithic monuments in Wessex as an index against which to read off changes in social complexity. What was important was that the sequence showed an increase in the scale of monuments, and thus in the amount of labour involved. From long barrow to enclosure to henge and Silbury Hill, there were a series of quantitative leaps. For Renfrew, these trends reflected the emergence of chiefdoms, political structures with a measure of hereditary authority that could co-ordinate and control the necessary labour.

These changes in scale over the longer term are important, but the approach was not without its problems. It missed the length of time that it took for a monument to reach the form that we see today. For many enclosures, the duration of that task varied from a generation to several centuries. This makes gross calculations of effort rather misleading and leaves unanswered the question of how labour was organised. The approach also assumed that the authority of certain people was a given before monuments were established. It made few concessions to the possibility that enclosures were arenas in which identity and authority were brought into being. The elevated and distanced vantage of these calculations also made it difficult to capture how a place worked in relation to people as they cut ditches or crossed causeways. It fostered a sense of the plan as a coherent design, a goal that was consciously and continuously worked towards. Establishing an enclosure for the first time, those who laboured may well have had a shared vision of the place they were creating. Sometimes they worked to incorporate prominent features into boundaries – escarpments, rock outcrops, ridges and watercourses. Plans could also be imposed upon topography, ignoring rather than respecting the immediate form of the land. However, the act of building was often patchy, varied and confused and this could become more marked as places were reworked over time. Chris Evans' suggestion that many enclosures were projects, abandoned rather than finished, could not be more apposite.

Where were enclosures established? Existing woodland clearings were places to which people had travelled before. They bore traces of a human past in the open ground and in the surrounding underwood. A few, like Windmill Hill, had seen settlement and even burial close at hand. Just as querns, midden and other durable tools marked prior occupation, so the ancestors of particular people could be a physical presence. Other clearings had seen use for limited camps or as raw material sources, places which had long histories before the first ditch was cut. This seems to have been the case at Maiden Castle, where flint outcrops exist on site. In Sussex too, there is a general correspondence with flint sources, although it is difficult to determine the significance of this pattern. Perhaps, like other sources, these were already places of communal and ancestral significance.

The same may also hold where enclosures were located with reference to other landscape features. Perhaps certain rock outcrops or ridges were prominent in social memory and in local myth. Where rivers served also to define perimeters, it may be that this boundary had a dual role. It was both a barrier to movement, and thus a threshold, and a medium for communication, an open path between places and perhaps between worlds. The importance of water as a source of fertility and as an agent of transformation would not have been lost on people at the time. That may be part of the reason why it was an appropriate medium for funerary rites and other offerings. Built close to rivers, or incorporating water into their boundaries, enclosures such as Southwick and Abingdon may well have drawn upon important origin myths and ancestral connections through the fact of their location.

There is much scope here for speculation. What is clear is that many enclosures were situated on seasonal thresholds, located between areas of settlement. Set apart, they were encountered in the context of broader cycles of movement and the husbandry of stock. They involved departures from the usual roll-call of daily experience. On occasion, the journey and the place fostered a sense of liminality, of being apart from the conventional order of things. Enclosures occupied specific times as well as places. They linked cycles of movement to cycles in nature and, as such, provided a focus for addressing important thresholds in people's lives.

The dramatic qualities of these settings would have been appreciated even before the first circuit was marked out. Used to a world where space and time can seem compressed, it is easy for us to miss the impact of coming to a place in the company of so many people. Where life routinely involved contacts with kin and a few relative strangers, an enclosure was a time and place where horizons could be rolled back. Arriving at a clearing at certain times, close kin would have been confronted by a crowd that jarred with everyday sensibilities. Sometimes the numbers ran into hundreds. There were people that they knew well, kin from neighbouring valleys and hills and those routinely met in the course of the seasonal round. There were others seen less frequently, at sources or at tombs. And there were those who seemed more distant, less-familiar faces and voices, the difference also marked, perhaps, by the clothes

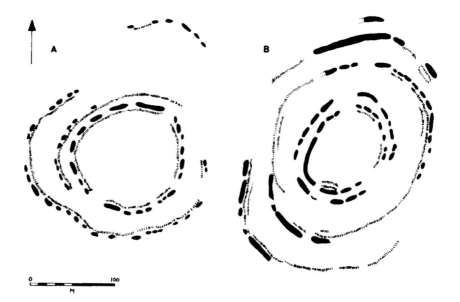

Figure 38 A. The Trundle, Sussex. B. Whitehawk, Sussex.

that they wore or the tools that they carried. There would have been animals too, herds mingled and confused in ways that broke with routine. No doubt people could recognise individual animals on sight, but it is possible that brands or other markings may have added to the sense of fragments brought together. As events unfolded, the area and the pattern of people would become more immediately familiar. The geography of a larger region could be mapped in this space between the trees. Hearths scattered across the open ground, a sense of fluidity and energy in the social order of things. The simple act of coming together reworked the social boundaries of routine life.

These conditions were brought into sharper focus as people worked. Many tasks were no different to those undertaken from day to day – cutting back clearings, removing scrub, maintaining the ground in various ways. What was different was the company in which those tasks were undertaken and their goal. Analogous to the clearings of many settlements, albeit on a different scale, these tasks created a core for a broader cultural group. That core was dramatic indeed, a white scar on the chalk, a vivid contrast on the gravel, elevated lines of posts and other timber settings. Particular tasks also required people to work in specific arrangements. At sites like Haddenham, Roughton, Icomb and Orsett, there was the felling of trees and the working of timbers for use in palisades. Some of the axe flakes near these and other sites reflect damage sustained by tools as people worked to produce the elements of such structures. These acts not only transformed the surrounding area, they also required co-operation, discussion and the sharing of burdens, the expending of effort in a collective endeavour.

Just how specific tasks were organised is difficult to determine. Discussions of design and laying out were probably held by elders from different lines and perhaps by ritual specialists. People may have worked most closely with their kin on certain tasks, labouring side by side with more distant cousins on others. We get a sense of these arrangements in the ditches on many sites, features cut with antler picks and the shoulder blades of cattle, with digging sticks and stone. These vary in character from chains of pits and short, segmented lines, to more massive, lengthy ditches. Although many have been truncated by heavy ploughing, some were originally no more than waist deep. Others were cut above head height, their scale enhanced by internal banks and allied structures. Parallels for the segmentary character of these features can be seen in the ditches around a number of earlier Neolithic tombs.

These patterns hint at the order of things during working. Construction may have been a collective act, participated in by all who gathered on a hill or near a river. Those with a certain standing may have co-ordinated kin as they worked timber or cut earth. Digging itself may have been preceded by observances from elders, but the company was also divided in other ways. The literature talks of ditches being 'gang dug', as if each segment or group of segments were the preserve of a specific body of people. In other words, the digging of different elements within a circuit was the customary responsibility

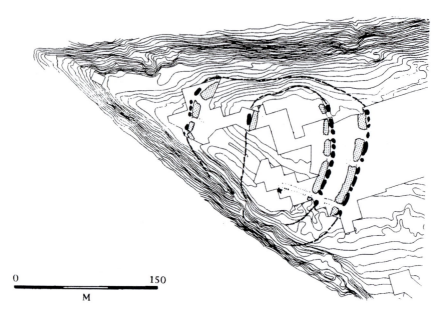

0   150
M

Figure 39 Crickley Hill, Gloucestershire: Phase 1b (after Dixon 1988).

of particular kin within the broader collective. A similar pattern of work may help us to understand variations along the line of certain stone-built enclosures. At Gardom's Edge, the rubble bank defining the site varies markedly. Elements of a stone facade are visible at certain points, massive uprights that retained a rubble core. In other places, the bank was simply a pile of gritstone boulders. The nature of the bank also changes on either side of certain causeways. The later reuse of stone might account for some of these differences, but a few at least suggest a variety in the people responsible for building and adding to this site over time.

There are dangers in taking this idea of gang digging too far. Many sites were reworked over time and this often involved a significant change in the character of circuits. Yet ditches were often dug, backfilled and re-dug on several occasions. At sites like Briar Hill and Staines these original features were respected and reconstituted. Such a task would have been easy where earthworks, posts or changes in vegetation marked the line of old circuits, but the simple fact of this observance suggests that the pattern of work and the pattern of the ditches held a particular significance for people at the time. They signified ideas about the constitution of the social group who came together. Often begun as circuits of pits, they brought a practice observed at the local scale and linked it to those of other lines. A shared tradition created a communal monument. Participation in ditch digging alongside others created a sense of the collective. The broader group was built by these acts. Yet the whole comprised a series of discrete elements. These were the products of work by specific families or even lineages, and this suggests a parallel concern with more local senses of identity. Scattered for much of the year, different families acknowledged their membership of the collective by gathering and through participation. They sustained a sense of difference through association with particular features.

These different themes were sustained over time. The drama of a gathering would have been remembered long after people had dispersed. When a handful of kin passed earthworks and clearings or camped nearby, the ground bore witness to signal events. As they watched over their cattle or talked around a fire, memory brought larger numbers and the past into focus. There were probably even occasions when small groups returned to particular features to undertake more localised rites. As the seasons turned, memories and local understandings were added to by further gatherings. New growth was cleared and old circuits were redefined. Chalk or gravel fill in ditches was removed, exposing features cut in the previous year or by an earlier generation. Re-digging, rediscovery and revelation went hand in hand. Practical traditions were maintained and it was through this rhetoric of reconstitution that the social histories and values of a place were renewed. Working brought the order of the cultural landscape into sharp relief; practical tradition added weight to the form.

Time and place

So far I have concentrated on the act of gathering, suggesting that digging itself sometimes took on the qualities of performance. I have said little of the events enclosures witnessed and their relation to political geographies, nor the purposes served by acts of deposition within their bounds. These form the focus of

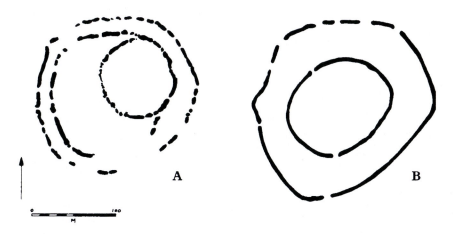

Figure 40 A. Briar Hill, Northamptonshire. B. Robin Hood's Ball, Wiltshire.

chapter 11. My concern has been simply to suggest something of the character and variety of enclosures and their location in the landscapes of the time.

Various conditions prompted people to work the idea of enclosure into certain valleys and hills. The renewal of relations with the past and with others was a constant, open-ended process. Just as many tombs bound people to the land and to their line, enclosures signified the loose federation of more varied kin. They were uncommon ground held in common. Such concerns were far from new. The gatherers and hunters of earlier millennia recognised similar issues as they met on the coast, at stone sources or by rivers at certain seasons. What was changing was the sense of tenure people recognised and the climate of ideas they inhabited. The scale and direction of routine activity involved contact, compromise and even conflict. As time passed, the genealogies attached to different parts of the landscape grew longer and more complex. The histories of different lines became more sedimented. Stock husbandry itself brought a different shape to the land and, like cultivation, raised changing concerns. The fertility of animals and crops, the debt owed to older generations and the obligation held to the future of the line. Local authority could also be dependent on ties with distant kin and thus on networks of trade and exchange. Competition between lineages in these changing conditions brought a new dynamic to relations between groups. Beyond everything else, the ancestors themselves had ranged far and wide and this meant the recognition of a political geography that was greater than any particular line.

Like the uptake of domesticates, this process had an almost inexorable and unseen quality. As one generation succeeded another and as people and ideas moved, ancestral rites and political discourse coalesced around the idea of enclosure. An arena, a spiritual perimeter, a focus for culture within nature; a monument that curved around a hill just as settlement turned around the edge or along the line of a clearing. Bounded places and times at which people could come together to face important and even dangerous concerns; dealings with the dead and with ancestors, dealings with strangers and all that was distant. Through that simple act, a sense of the collective was grounded in the past. Dispersed communities recognised a greater order through these places. Through them, they made and remade the ties that are manifest in shared material traditions.

Enclosures were just one manifestation of this process. The earlier Neolithic saw the development of other monumental traditions which served overlapping roles. These included cursus monuments which varied in length from a few hundred metres to several kilometres. Often associated with human remains and sometimes built to incorporate existing long barrows, these enigmatic sites had a close association with ancestral rites. Linked by alignments to movements in the heavens, rites at these places evoked the ties that stretched between the living and the spirit world. Communities who gathered and worked to build these sites would have been left in no doubt as to the strength of those ties, nor the authority of those who could speak with the world beyond. Tied as it was to the heavens, the order of things seemed beyond question.

Complex alignments can also be seen at other monuments. At Godmanchester in Cambridgeshire, a cursus was aligned on the edge of a massive, rectangular enclosure. Placed within the perimeter of the site were massive posts, aligned so as to highlight solstice and equinox. These timbers were cut and set in place around 3800 BC. Here too, assembled companies may have sought spiritual help in renewing the fertility of the land, their dead caught up in these observances. Caught up in the company of others, they could also address other concerns.

These different monuments reflect the regionally varied ways in which scattered communities acknowledged their place in a broader social and ancestral world. They brought people together in cycles that took their form from the turning of the seasons. They created arenas for a variety of meetings and rites. But differences in form and associations suggest that there was more than one way in which the past and present order of things could be acknowledged. These traditions were not mutually exclusive. Enclosures were some of the first large monuments to appear, but cursuses were constructed while some were still in use. The two types of monument were often set apart, but some cursuses were established and used in the same areas as enclosures. A few were even cut across the boundaries of older sites, suggesting shifts in the practices through which social relations were reproduced.

Despite their scale, there is no reason to assume that these places were built simply to celebrate the political standing of particular individuals or lineage heads. The authority of some may certainly have been recognised. But this was not singular and was just one theme to be acknowledged as people worked or attended important rites. In the relatively fluid political conditions of the time, a season or a generation often saw that standing rise and fall, shifting back and forth between different lines.

With time, this situation changed. Monuments brought important forces together. Their use sustained the idea of an order beyond the hearths of a particular line. More than this, they captured ancestral rites, exchange and the broader social landscape in a single moment. Here things were laid bare, experienced with a clarity that was simply impossible in the company of close kin alone. That clarity was also potential. Enclosures created the conditions under which new forms of political authority could be articulated through control of the rites they contained. As they brought the collective into focus, enclosures became resources for the realisation of inequalities.

10 Drawing the line

The girl sat patiently by the embers, damping the heat with a scatter of fresh earth. She leaned and tapped the vessel lying at the centre, flicking it as she would a heifer who strayed from the track. It sounded whole; no fracture yet.

Her uncle had shown her the way in this making. The trick for good resin was to peel the white bark with the strongest smell. Pliant and tacky, the smell stayed on the hands for days. You could chew the resin to make it work, but it was better to heat it slowly, to take time. Satisfied that all was well, she looked up to take in all that turned around her. She was not yet used to the sight of so many.

She had arrived the day before. Coming to the clearing with cattle and close kin, she found most of the company already gathered. They had watched the smoke on the horizon for much of the previous day. Taking the form of a line while distant, the trails from the fires resolved into a circle along the edge of the trees. Now they were settled on the margins, finding their place among the clan. The girl's eyes followed the smoke from her fire. The view took her back along the path they had taken and out across the forest to more distant hills. The clearings of earlier years, the pastures of others, the rise that held the good stone. Tracks along which their lives had unfolded and climbs that made sense only at a distance. The story of their line ranged far and wide. Those who knew the story never lost their way.

She had been this way before: the first time soon after her birth, the second when she had seen ten summers; once on her mothers' back, once on foot for her initiation. Three more years had passed since then. This time she came to the circle as one of the company of adults.

The circle brought everything together. It took all that was distant and drew it close. Lines were joined, scattered herds became one. There were welcome faces and those hardly seen; cattle with varied hides. She counted eight different cuts on their ears. Even the souls were gathering. Approaching, she had listened to sounds that gained variety with each passing step. Summoned by the open ground, the birds sang with the voices of those who watched over the clan. Their descendants were all around her in the clearing, talking, working, gathering wood and news.

Heating slowly in the pot, the resin grew heavy. She lifted the leather cover to test the brew, dipping a twig into the darkness. This was the best way. Raised on end, the twig would show if all was well. If the resin ran easily down the wood it needed more time. If it stayed near the tip it was ready. The timing had to be just right, or the brew would set too well and there would not be time to work. Right now it needed more time, perhaps a while. It was still no thicker than honey.

Wiping the twig, the girl turned back to look at those who worked nearby. Many had begun to cut the ground along the line of the old posts; a pace on either side. Already the earth was white along most of the perimeter, the small knot of her family unravelled along the line. She would join them when the brew was done. They worked carefully, antler and axe following the edge where the loose earth met the chalk. The rise and fall of bodies repeated itself around the circle. Others followed with bone and basket, collecting the spoil and heaving it up to form the inner face of the line.

Her kin had paused in the digging and were huddled close to the ground. She stretched to catch their words. They had come to the end of the ditch and were talking of the vessel before them. Laid at the base when whole, it had since returned to earth, the fire taken back from the clay. Like many of the bones and flakes that lay scattered on the banks, she did not know when it had been buried. Perhaps it had always been there.

Her father knew. The vessel went back to when his father's bones had been raised, when he had given meat to all the clan. That had been a powerful time. He wondered aloud if there were any who could remember better. Like the remains of the feast, it had been set to give thanks to the souls who had guided his herds that year. They had kept all the calves until the last of the frost and saw to it that few were lost. With their help and that of his brothers, he had gained much respect from the gift. Raising his axe, he pulled a little chalk back into the ditch to cover the soft clay. As it fell, the chalk brought with it a few small fragments of a child's skull. No one noticed. The earth was rich with bone and with the ghosts of their line.

Digging continued on the other side of the entrance. One of her aunts and four of her cousins bent to the task. Raising chalk and earth, they added to the weave of her fathers' tale with threads of their own. Talk ranged widely; across the years and the generations that were held in the circle. It touched on the summer that had been and on the winter that would follow soon. There was rich stock here, good meat for the feasts that would start the next day and for the trading that came later. Her cousins had already visited the scattered hearths. They had seen the fine stone and some of the goods brought by others. Their talk was full of guesses as to who would make the most powerful gifts. There would be much to eat and to watch once the dead had been raised.

The girl turned back to her task. Raising the cover once more, she dipped then held the twig on end. The resin stayed, reluctant to leave the tip. She called to her uncle and her mother, the tone of her voice a signal that it was time. The resin would hold the men's costumes when they danced but it was also for her. In two days she would marry, taking her line into the valleys that ran down the far side of the hills. It was a good match. There had been no arguments, and the distant cousin who would be her husband seemed happy at the prospect of sharing her hearth. Besides, he would bring many cattle when he came, meat for the winter and for gatherings in the years to come. Once the costumes were complete, she would help in the digging. After that, she and the other women would go back to the forest to prepare.

Great Wilbraham.

Knap Hill.

Figure 41

11 Arenas of value

During the 1980s, the extension of quarrying near Peterborough brought a complex of prehistoric monuments under threat. One of these, Etton, was the subject of one of the more complete excavations yet undertaken on a causewayed enclosure. The site lay on gravel close to the river, one of a pair of enclosures separated by water. It exists now only as archive, a monument in plans and cardboard boxes.

Water brought a pattern to activities at Etton. Situated on low ground, it was prone to inundation from adjacent watercourses. It may have been flooded from time to time, parts of the site acquiring a blanket of fine silts. The circle of the seasons also saw areas turn to marsh and there were ditch segments that may have contained standing water. Patterns of use reflected that fluidity. Permanent occupation is difficult to trace, and much of the evidence makes more sense as a result of diverse and episodic events.

The archive is rich, reflecting a monument born of collective endeavour that was reworked over time. Pollen from the ditches suggests that the environs of the site were already clear before digging began, used for stock and the growing of crops. These ditches were recut on several occasions, the whole emphasised and renewed by those who gathered. Silt scraped back and gravel edges exposed. Many became repositories for a rich array of placed deposits, patterned in ways that seem strange from our vantage in the present. Ditch segments were also re-dug and modified at irregular intervals, as if different elements could move in and out of focus independently of each other. The site was also bisected by a narrow ditch, leading Francis Pryor to suggest a division into two symbolic zones, one associated with the living, the other with the dead.

Waterlogging has led to the preservation of materials that are often absent from more well-drained sites. Coppice stools were identified on the perimeter and there is abundant evidence for the working of underwood and timber. Tools and pottery are present in some numbers, the stone extracted from the local gravels, clays from sources not yet known. There are 'exotic' tools as well, axes made from Cumbrian stone that show signs of deliberate smashing and formal burial. These were deposited in the ditches and in some of the pits that pock-marked the interior. The ditches also contained

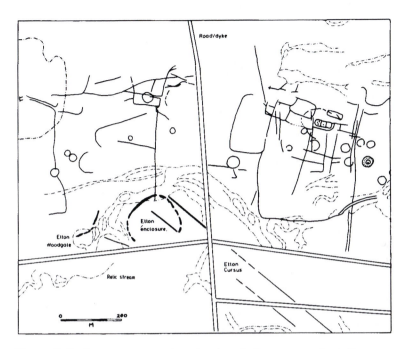

Figure 42 Enclosure, cursus and predominantly later cropmarks at Etton,
Cambridgeshire.

fragments of people and animals. There are bundles of cattle bone placed in
ditches while still fresh. Some may still have held flesh when buried. Fragments of people were often treated in a similar manner, but there are also
human bones which were overlooked. Scattered unnoticed from one part of
the enclosure to another, these were weathered and gnawed at by dogs.

It is difficult to make sense of this material. The residues of formal
moments lie cheek by jowl with traces of domestic activity, an amalgam of
ritual and routine. There is an entanglement of roles and values, as if different
qualities of the monument were pulled in and out of focus over time. Prosaic
patterns reiterated from one year to the next and more performative events,
space becoming sacred at certain times. Variety and change in the details of
features also suggest a place that was significant at several scales, a pivot for a
broad collective, an arena for activities that emphasised only part of the
whole.

Crossing the line

The digging and marking of many enclosure perimeters mapped a broad
social geography. Some, like Etton, may have witnessed limited residence or
periods of occupation nearby, but even here, there were moments when a

Figure 43 Primary ditch deposits at Etton. In the foreground is a dump of pyre material, behind that a human skull accompanied by *Bos* bones, beyond that a rock resting on top of potsherds and, in the distance, arranged deposits of organic material. (Photo: Francis Pryor.)

broader company assembled. This map was committed to memory as people moved around the margins of these sites collecting wood or food and visiting other hearths. Others perhaps camped further afield, drawing close only when the time was right. On this frame were woven the stories of all that went on from one hearth or one valley to another. There were opportunities for exchange, for the creation of new bonds and for talk, for the passing on of local, seasonal, histories that ran into one another. Perspective was different at these times.

What gave those gatherings their form were the circuits cut into chalk or gravel, the perimeters defined by earth and timber. Testaments to a communion through labour, these perimeters carried many connotations. Similar to the pits dug on settlements, ditch segments could be a focus for a sense of the local. Here, however, they were far from dispersed. They were linked to contain an area and this created a threshold of broader and more signal importance.

What did it mean to cross this line? Given a pattern of periodic use, there would have been times when it was observed in the breach. People and animals crossed backfilled or open ditches on their way elsewhere, pausing only to camp before moving on. There would be memory of course, and where the presence of ancestors was keenly felt, perhaps respect or even fear. But the monuments were dormant at these times, their edges and their meanings blurred.

In the company of many, when the earth was freshly cut, that simple step could take on a different character. These were thresholds across which things could change. Multiple causeways convey a sense of permeability, of people moving in and out. Entry meant crossing between the terminals of two ditches, and these were sometimes the focus for offerings. At sites like Etton itself, timber settings or gateways emphasised passage across the boundary. At Melbourn and Orsett, palisades would have had a similar effect. People approaching were presented with a barrier and with the possibility of crossing the line at specified points.

Not all entrances were the same. Some are wider than others and there are many which lack any embellishment or outworking. A few have wider or in-turned ditch terminals, emphasising the depth of the threshold crossed by people and animals. During important events, there was a protocol to the pattern of entry. At Briar Hill, Offham and Staines, particular thresholds had to be crossed. There are also sites like Haddenham, where the curve of the enclosure is flattened on one side. These facades again suggest a particular approach to the monument. People had to process, bringing a formality to their movement before they even reached the line. When causeways were reached, movement became tighter. There would be an order to the act of crossing. Some would move in front of others and at certain moments, this meant an acknowledgement of seniority and difference. That acknowledge-ment may have also come from exclusion. For some events, age or gender may have determined rights of access, entry a hallmark of inclusion in particular companies. Where major entrances were opposed, protocol could extend to choreographed movement by different groups of men or women, or perhaps different kin. We should not assume that the frame of these places created only one order among people.

Multiple circuits at sites like Abingdon or Whitehawk took this distinction even further. It is not always clear whether circuits were added over time but, even when this was the case, additions were often made at the scale of a few generations rather than centuries. Like the digging of old ditches, the form of a place was reiterated through the addition of concentric rings. Respect for the original core meant respect for the past, an acknowledgement of the histories behind particular gatherings. But the effect was to deepen the threshold and to multiply boundaries that could divide and differentiate people. Perhaps some could progress only to a certain point during important ceremonies, while others were free to move to the centre of things. This would have been particularly clear where important causeways were aligned

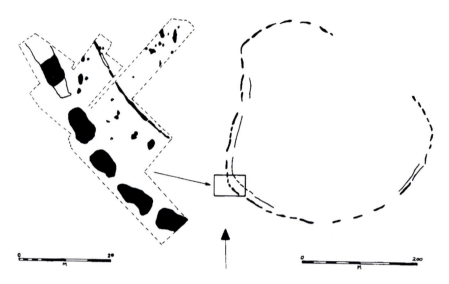

Figure 44 Haddenham, Cambridgeshire (after Evans 1988).

across different circuits, a pattern maintained at Offham and Windmill Hill, among others.

Passage across these thresholds also constituted a movement between arenas of value. The line drew a distinction between the world outside and that which lay within. It brought culture to the core and opposed itself to the world beyond. A world of natural and spiritual forces and a land that was ordered by the histories and aspirations of different lines. Forces to be contained or called upon, commonalities and tensions to be attended to. Outside was the everyday. Though rich in ancestry and history, this was a world shaped by obligation and by tenurial claim. Conventions on access shaped movement and work, creating an order and sometimes friction in relations between communities. Inside, values changed. Usual patterns of encounter were suspended as people came together. A sense of being apart from the common order of experience lent a weight to events and to dealings with others. Different regimes of value overlapped in these places, and this shaped both the character and the content of various transactions.

What went on when the line was crossed? Inventories from excavations speak of a variety in activities, some prosaic, others more formal. There is evidence for the working and the use of stone – debris from flaking and tools such as scrapers, serrated flakes and blades, even fragments of querns and polissoirs, their faces polished from the sharpening of axes. Sometimes the balance of an assemblage is revealing. At Briar Hill, tools occur in some numbers, evidence of a rich mix of tasks. Scrapers, retouched flakes and blades are common, yet the volume of waste material is relatively low, as if the working of stone took place elsewhere, people bringing tools and cores with them when they assembled. At Maiden Castle, the situation is rather different. Like Briar Hill and Etton, there are tools in some numbers. Yet there is also a large volume of waste, some of it reflecting the working of stone that outcropped on or near to the site. Evidence for a significant volume of working has also been identified at Offham. At Maiden Castle, much of this material reflects the dressing and working of cores from which flakes and blades could be struck. The remainder is composed of distinctive flakes struck from stone in the making of larger tools such as axes.

On other sites with multiple circuits there are hints that the areas defined by specific boundaries were inhabited in different ways. The innermost circuits were often the first to be cut, and these can show the greatest evidence for redigging over time. They can also contain the largest numbers of artefacts, some deposited with care. At Abingdon, for example, the inner ditch enclosed a space used for a number of specialised rites. The outer circuit defined an area which shows signs of occupation. One reading of this pattern would be that multiple rings focussed attention on an inner core of particular importance, and that passage towards the centre involved increasing the distance between participants and the outside world. Camped or established inside the outer circuit, inhabitants were also protected, but remained set apart from the focus of more dramatic events.

It is tempting to take the evidence from Abingdon as typical, and a similar argument has been made for Briar Hill. Unfortunately, the evidence is not that simple. Often there were shifts in the use of different zones over time. There are also cases, like Windmill Hill, where the situation is reversed. Human bone occurs in considerable densities in the outer ditch, as it does at Whitehawk. The strongest evidence for some form of occupation comes from the innermost area. Other features add further grey tones to these otherwise black-and-white patterns. At many sites, segments within different circuits can display a variety of form and content impossible to reconcile with a simple division of significance between inner and outer rings. Progression to a core was important at certain moments, and boundaries could be signal markers of that journey. But there was no one pattern to the way that the spaces within different enclosures were used. Individual elements within outer or intermediate circuits could also become the focus for specialised activities. At Etton, segments were re-dug at different times, and this suggests that at least some enclosures could be places of local ceremonial after larger companies had dispersed.

Death and exchange

What do particular deposits tell us about the nature of those activities? These are varied in the extreme, although they echo some of the material found in the forecourts and ditch terminals at a number of barrows. Some are the products of casual circumstance, material swept or scuffed into hollows, passing unnoticed into the ground. Some are elements from middens that eroded into features soon after they were cut, traces of occupation from an earlier time. There were also the residues from living and working both during and after the time when particular enclosures were maintained. Short-term, seasonal and sometimes more concerted, the remnants of these camps are well represented where ditches remained open, weathering and silting up of their own accord.

Things were often different. Many deposits show signs of intent and design, offerings placed and buried in a single moment. Some were placed soon after ditches were first cut. These include clusters of arrowheads and non-local axes, their sources more than a month's walk away. Pottery too can be exotic, like the vessels made with Cornish Gabbroic clays found at Hambledon Hill and other sites in the south-west. These vessels could enter ditches while still whole, perhaps with contents offered to the earth. At other times, the vessel itself was the focus. At Etton, complete pots were inverted on the base of a ditch, that position a denial of their use as containers. Carved chalk objects

Figure 45 Skull in ditch at Hambledon Hill. (Photo: Roger Mercer.)

could also be included. At Windmill Hill, four chalk phalluses hint that deposition was sometimes tied to ideas of fertility and biological as well as social renewal. There are also nests of knapping debris that can be completely refitted, as if it was the creative act, rather than a product, which was the object of attention. Other deposits incorporate animal bones, most often cattle, and there are pockets of ash and organic residues that are the remains of fires and food consumed elsewhere on site. At Haddenham some of these ashes were placed on a mat in the bottom of the ditch. Fragments of people and even complete burials are common too. Patterned deposition is a common element across sites with more than one circuit, and structured deposits have been recovered from pits in the interior of many.

As Isobel Smith noted in the 1960s, it is simplistic to treat these assemblages as evidence for settlement. For her, the pattern and structure of many deposits suggested a concern with 'ritual rubbish', material brought from other sites to be buried during elaborate fertility rites. Elements of this argument can now be questioned, but the spirit of her suggestion still remains. These deposits often reflect distinct episodes of consumption that were brought to a close by the burial of particular residues. Set apart from the everyday, these episodes involved people, animals and materials drawn from different communities and different regimes of value.

Often clustered in the terminals of ditches and near important thresholds, these deposits were passed when people moved in and out of an enclosure. Visible when placed or after redigging, or even simply remembered, these offerings established certain themes and values as a presence. These were acknowledged when people crossed the line. Strung together by oral tradition, offerings allowed people to work a variety of associations into these places. These values could also be added to. At both Etton and Hambledon Hill vertical patterning in some ditch sections reveals the maintenance of traditions of formal deposition over time.

Different deposits could mean different things, though many contributed to a sense of the collective. Freshly butchered joints and other meaty parts of animals suggest that feasting was particularly important. Beef seems to have been particularly favoured, but there is plentiful evidence for the consumption of pork and mutton. Charcoal from vinewood at Hambledon Hill may also reflect yet another form of celebration. The sharing of meat from valued animals was one expression of the ties that bound different groups together. Like building, it helped to make those ties, and where the provision of food was also a means of gaining standing among others, feasts could be a focus for competition. At a time when the capacity to give was as important as accumulation, to be honoured with food was to be placed in debt. To feed many people at an important event was to gain a certain standing and renown.

These moments when people gave and shared food were commemorated through acts of interment. Bones and joints were gathered together and placed along the bases and in the terminals of ditches. Occasionally the heads

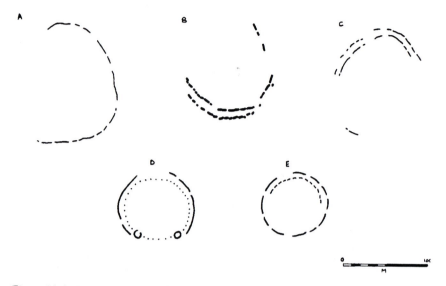

Figure 46 A. Etton. B. Upton. C. Uffington. D. Melbourn. E. Roughton.

themselves would be treated in this manner, just like the heads of certain people. Here too the close identification of people and animals was acknowledged. Those who participated fixed the memory and significance of events through this act. They also brought proceedings to a close. Consumption confirmed the status of cattle as sources and expressions of standing. Drawn from particular herds, their bones acknowledged both the character and the direction of the gift given by one line to another. Over time, these ditches received other dumps from different events. Taken together, these bones came from more than one herd and their presence in ditches embodied the collective nature of earlier assemblies. For those who came after, oral tradition and observation allowed these deposits to be read as a record of earlier gatherings and the relations they involved.

Feasting may be an end in itself, but often it accompanies other acts. At enclosures it was often caught up in elaborate rites of passage, events that surrounded important thresholds in people's lives. Rites of passage frequently possess a tripartite structure. An initial stage of *separation* gives way to a period of *liminality* and this in turn is followed by a process of *reincorporation*. Thresholds between these stages can be subject to strict proscriptions. This is often vital, because such occasions involve ideas about the order of things in the social and natural worlds. They expose that order to the threat of chaos and change. Separation from the world of everyday associations and the creation of liminal conditions suspends usual conventions and contains that threat. The final stage of reincorporation confirms familiar frameworks of classification and order.

Figure 47 Skull in ditch at Maiden Castle, Dorset. (Photo: Niall Sharples.)

Funerary ritual is a common context in which rites of passage may come to the fore, a reflection of the need to make sense of death, to rationalise mortality in a broader scheme of things. For communities of the earlier Neolithic, these themes cohered in ancestral rites around contemporary tombs. They were present when bones were scattered, or when they circulated as relics in different settings, and they were present at enclosures. Death and the continuity of life were paramount concerns for those who assembled, but death had many stages and forms, and these were acknowledged by a variety in the treatment accorded to corpses. Many deposits contain parts of bodies that were broken and scattered. There are also complete burials of men, women and children. Skulls are particularly well represented and were often the focus for formal deposits. Lines of skulls were placed along the bottom of ditches at Hambledon Hill, while at Etton they were linked with other offerings. Skulls or skull fragments have been identified in pits and ditches at many sites and it is possible that some were buried as heads rather than bare bones. Marks on a cranium from the outer ditch at Staines suggest the active severing of the head before time and decay could play a part.

The fragmented and scattered character of human bones has led many to conclude that enclosures occupied specific positions within rites of passage. At Hambledon Hill, Roger Mercer interpreted the central area of the enclosure as a zone in which bodies were transformed by defleshing. Left to rot or actively stripped, he saw corpses broken down to their constituent elements in this area. Death dominates his account and it is easy to understand why. Beyond the lines of skulls, the site contained fragments of many men and women. The bones of children are particularly common and there are even burials of the very young. The evidence led Mercer to describe the main enclosure as a 'reeking necropolis' whose 'awful silence was broken only by the din of crows'.

The evidence from Hambledon is particularly dramatic, but it echoes that found on many sites. Whatever other purposes they served, many enclosures offered a place and a time where the bodies of the dead could be broken. Exposed on platforms or buried for a while in pits, bodies would begin to lose their flesh, their features returning to the sky or to the earth. Birds and other animals may have helped in this process and active defleshing may have been undertaken when people came together. In these cases, the signs and the smells of decay brought a dramatic quality to the process of transformation. Flesh corrupted but bones were clean. Like the ancestors, they persisted. We know little about the order of things during these events. The cleaning of excavated bodies may have been a prerogative of close kin. It may have also been overseen by ritual specialists, those well placed to mediate the passage of the dead between different states of being.

On occasion, this was a prerequisite to their use elsewhere. Inventories from enclosures and tombs have a complementary character, and this suggests that bones may have circulated between these settings. When this happened, exposure at an enclosure served a specific purpose. It took an individual who was known and recognised, perhaps respected and even loved, and turned that person into a collection of bones. As flesh decayed, personal biography faded. In its place, it was possible to conceive of the deceased as a member of the ancestral community. Perhaps it was out of the mess and confusion of this process that a few bones were scattered, only to become crushed and

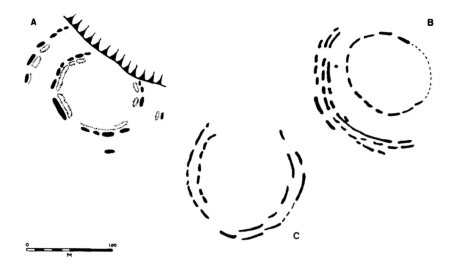

Figure 48 A. Coombe Hill. B. Orsett. C. Great Wilbraham.

splintered in the jaws of dogs. Once relics had been selected, other elements lost much of their significance.

Enclosures also made it possible to contain the chance event of death itself. Bodies could be kept within their bounds until the cycle had turned to the appropriate time for funerary and ancestral rites. When the time was right and the proper company had gathered, decayed bodies could be taken from a platform or unearthed from a pit to continue on their journey. Released from their flesh, they could inhabit the world as spirits. Physically marginal and socially liminal, enclosures provided the proscribed conditions in which it was possible to approach the dead, to transform them and harness their powers as ancestral forces and, where death brought changes in obligation and alliance, the communal setting of these rites made it possible to establish a new and different order. The drama and the threat of death was contained and subsumed within the greater pattern; continuity and renewal were assured.

These were places of transition for the dead, just as they were for the living, but this involved more than the creation of bones to be carried away. Fragments and burials on many sites suggest a different quality to the connection. Buried in ditches and close to thresholds, bones also bound scattered communities to a monument and to each other. They strengthened the links between particular families and specific ditch segments, some of which were visited again when the company had scattered. The bones of different lines were also held in relation to each other and this reinforced a sense of the whole. The map of the broader world was sanctioned by their presence and by the roots they put down. Crossing the line sharpened the memory of kin who had come to these places. Anchored by bones, their spirits were strong and it was here that they joined in communion with others. Their presence emphasised the continuity of the broader group across generations and they ensured its spiritual fertility. Distributed around perimeters, they also offered strength where enclosures were built to protect or to contain powerful forces. They were present to watch over events. Perhaps the heads that were sometimes buried retained their eyes to help in that regard.

The burial of bodies raises other possibilities. Some graves may have been intended as no more than temporary – a liminal stage in proceedings that persisted for far longer than planned. We can only guess as to why certain bodies were never recovered. Other graves were clearly designed as final resting places for the dead, an example being that recovered at Offham. Others have been identified at sites like Knap Hill, Staines and Whitehawk. Here the identities of specific people remained in focus while they were finally laid to rest, creating associations with specific lines that were powerful indeed. Why certain people were singled out for this treatment is difficult to determine. Some may have been bad deaths. Out of time or against nature in some way, the passing of certain people may have been perceived as a threat to the order of things. Because of this, their bodies and their spirits needed to be contained.

Patterns in burials suggest other themes at play. The sample is small, but what there is suggests an emphasis upon the burial of children. This is a

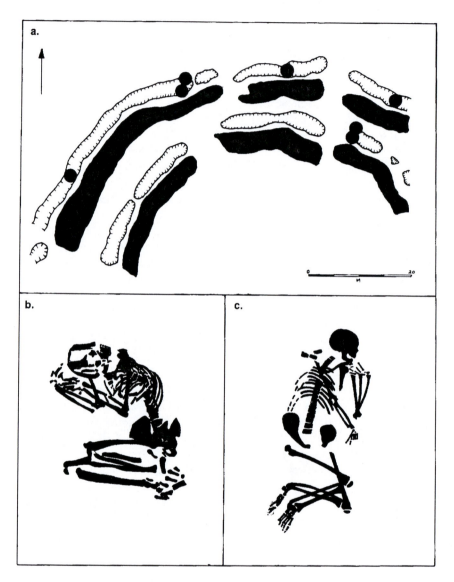

Figure 49 a. Association of human remains with ditchworks at Offham. b. Burial
from Offham. c. Burial from Staines.

particularly strong feature at Maiden Castle and Hambledon Hill. Women are
less well represented, with burials recorded at sites like Whitehawk, Abingdon
and Staines, the latter including a partial cremation. However, these burials do
outnumber those of men. There may be many reasons for these patterns.
Children may be present in some numbers because of their age. As infants or
juveniles, they had yet to undertake important rites of passage themselves.

They were not sufficiently socialised to enter the company of elders, let alone the community of the ancestors. Perhaps their burial in enclosures confirmed their liminal state, the monuments, in their turn, being added to by their presence. Perhaps they also offered the promise of rebirth. Women may have been buried because of their particular association with fertility and with the continuity of family lines. Where enclosures were concerned with the making and remaking of the social order, those associations may have been of some importance. They may also appear because of their connections to different families. The same could be equally true of men.

The significance of burial may have also changed. As the earlier Neolithic unfolded, long barrows increasingly became the focus for the burial of adult men. This was not an exclusive pattern, and it resolved itself over several centuries, but one reason for the interment of women at enclosures could have been this change in the associations of certain houses of the dead. On the basis of present evidence, this is open ground for interpretation. We should allow, however, that these varied themes were underpinned by the ties of kinship through which people had lived. While their memory was sustained, those ties remained as historical facts. This too may have increased in importance over time.

Rites associated with the dead also harnessed other materials. The bones of the dead were powerful, but equally important were some of the tools and trappings of their lives. At least some of the deposits of pottery and stone implements were linked to the passage of the dead into the ancestral realm. Axes are a good case in point, examples made of flint and from non-local stone occurring on many sites. At Carn Brea, Hembury, Hazard Hill and Maiden Castle these included axes made from Cornish gabbros. At Haddenham and Etton, axes made from Cumbrian (Langdale) tuff were identified during

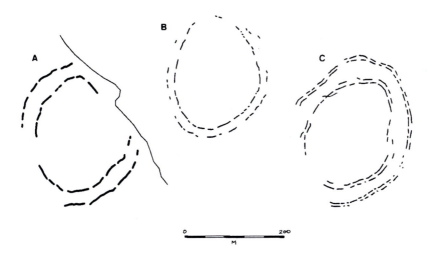

Figure 50 A. Southwick. B. Barholm. C. Northborough.

Figure 51 Animal bone in the ditch of Windmill Hill. Some of the deposits in the
  ditches on this site represent the gathering up of midden material. Others
  may have been laid down to mark the conclusion of important feasts or
  ceremonies. The bones of animals and people were sometimes placed
  together and there is evidence for the deliberate burial of several species,
  including dogs. (Photo: Alasdair Whittle.)

excavation. Sometimes the distances involved were even greater. Hambledon
Hill and High Peak both yielded axes made of jadeite, a stone which has its
source on the continent. Although these examples lack a secure context,
many axes were the subjects of formal acts of deposition in ditches and in pits.
At Etton, it is possible that axes were deliberately broken before burial. There
are other associations too. At Maiden Castle and Hambledon Hill, some of
the pits in which axes have been recovered may have been associated with the
exposure and defleshing of the dead.

   Why was it important to treat axes and other materials in this way? At a place
where the dead could be transformed, what was at issue was their social
identity. As men and women, they had occupied particular places in networks
of kinship, affiliation and obligation, that position sometimes marked by the
tools that they carried or acquired. Death brought changes in those relations
and in the significance of possessions. Certain tools had been given as gifts,
their passage cementing ties between groups. Others stood for roles and
responsibilities held in life and some were simply belongings. They carried
histories and biographies. Some could be handed on. But others 'stood for'
certain qualities of the dead and had to be reworked by burial and containment. Their treatment was a narrative that ran in parallel with the treatment
of corpses. The body of the axe or the pot might even be broken, just as flesh
and bone were disassembled. The inversion of vessels might have been in

keeping with similar themes. At Etton, Francis Pryor suggested that pots in these positions represented skulls that were also placed in ditches. If that was the case, then the analogy went further than form. Both were empty containers. Where burial was akin to planting, deposits were the seedcorn that ensured future continuity. Offered in the midst of death, they sustained the hope of rebirth.

There is no reason to assume that we can explain all deposits at enclosures by reference to the dead. Many were in keeping with the more general tradition of renewing tenure through offering and interment. Here, as elsewhere, they were anchors for local memory. In any case, death was just one of the thresholds at which social categories were brought into sharp relief. Marriage brought outsiders into existing kinship structures. It provided access to labour through children and through the obligations that ensued when different lines were joined. Proscriptions surrounded the passage to adulthood and again to the company of elders. In a world cut by tensions between age grades and kin, these thresholds were highly charged. They were best dealt with in contained and liminal settings. Enclosures had much to offer as places of initiation. They were also a logical setting for sanctioning social changes that arose through practices like marriage.

Initiation and marriage were probably marked in many ways, by inclusion in particular companies and by the passing on of restricted knowledge. Transition could also be effected by participation in a feast or in other practices. Sometimes, this involved specific forms of production. We have

Figure 52 A small axe from the Lake District deposited in a pit at Etton, near Peterborough. (Photo: Francis Pryor.)

already seen how several enclosures were located close to stone sources, places that had perhaps long been important. Occasionally we get glimpses that extraction and working may have been graded in some way. For example, the making of flint axes was well represented at Maiden Castle. Yet survey in the environs of the site has shown little or no evidence that these tools were also produced outside, even though raw material would have been available. Perhaps this reflects a distinction drawn by people at the time. Where production was geared to the making of tools that carried specific values and associations, it might also need to be contained. The drama of a gathering bestowed a particular significance on both person and product. This might also explain some of the knapping debris occasionally found in placed deposits. Where offerings were made at the conclusion of certain events, waste from working was an appropriate token to place in the earth.

There was another practice that was crucial to the crossing of many thresholds. At a time when identity and position were often expressed in the possession and use of things, initiation and the circulation of people were bound up in the circulation of goods. Exchange wove different lines together. It made relations that were worked and reworked over time and, as such, it was as political as it was practical. As places which brought people together, enclosures provided the conditions in which it was possible to undertake important transactions.

This link with exchange has long been acknowledged. Yet we often seem to miss the varied quality of transactions and their context, the manner in which exchange was articulated in people's lives. Some have talked of grand mono-

Figure 53 Cornish ground stone axe and pot deposited at Hambledon Hill, Dorset. (Photo: Roger Mercer.)

polies and trade, conjuring up a system that was both integrated and extensive. In this picture, elites hold sway over regions, directing the flow of goods and somehow profiting from that role. The system is often singular. What is lost is any sense of the mess of people dealing with others, the complex moral economies and the blurring of regimes of value at different scales. Distant people, ideas and artefacts; people who, in turn, extended contact even further afield; seasonal kin or those seen daily – a tangle of relations.

Transactions at these times took many forms. Camps established in the environs of enclosures brought scattered lines into close proximity. Here it was possible to meet and talk, to renew old ties and to settle new deals. As herds mingled on the edges of clearings, it would be possible to barter for new stock, to reach agreements about which bull would serve which heifers. The following spring, calves signifed the moment when a bond had been made or a debt paid. There was a history in these animals. Where rustling had brought tensions to the surface, this was a place and time where reparations could be made, the stock replaced or compensated for in other ways. Trading partners seen from time to time would also be present. Old obligations could be discharged and new plans drawn, agreements to help in clearing or in lifting stone. Bound up in many transactions were more overtly social themes, such as structures of alliance, of competition and debt. All had to be made and made again. Marriages would be proposed and discussed and those long planned enacted. Grievances could be aired or satisfied and new allegiances formed. Even at the most local of scales, these exchanges had a political quality. They remade ties between kin and others, they entwined different genealogies and reworked debts. Some transactions could happen elsewhere and at other times. But the context of proceedings lent even these a particular significance.

Other forms of exchange were more highly charged. Gift giving was a means of inflicting debt upon others. Caught up in marriage rites or in more overtly competitive displays between lineage heads, it provided a basis for prestige and renown. It had consequences for the authority that some held over others. Sometimes the gift was food. Through the provision of a feast, it was possible to celebrate and to anticipate reciprocation. Where food was given to ancestors, gifts placed in ditches or in pits reflected well on the giver. To place certain ancestors in one's debt was to generate symbolic capital. There were also artefacts that endured. Through what Annette Weiner calls *keeping while giving*, gifts that passed to others accrued obligations and a local deference. More than this, the gifts themselves acquired histories. They were reminders of obligations, and they held the spirit of the moment when they had moved from one line to another. When people dispersed, they carried those relations with them in material form.

Keeping while giving served a variety of purposes, but the relations it sustained were far from stable. The giving of gifts reformed as it renewed and this was a potential for change. Relations were easily undermined in the face of competition at various scales, among lineage heads or between elders and young adults. Movement also brought the possibility of new alliances and, as one generation gave way to another, the topography of the cultural landscape could shift. One of the hallmarks of this volatile regional politics was the use made of the exotic. The term should be used with caution. Artefacts from remote sources often moved in short steps, passing from hand to hand through different local systems. Sometimes they moved as commodities, at other times as gifts, their value dependent on the relationship between giver and receiver. But in a world that was local and dispersed, artefacts and ideas from remote sources could carry a particular significance. Distance itself was a powerful, yet malleable resource. Simply having knowledge of distant worlds and forces could engender respect.

These ideas may help us to understand why enclosures have a close association with non-local artefacts. What made these items important was not simply the remoteness of their sources, but the history of the hands through which they had passed. Many of the axes found on enclosures had travelled great distances before they were placed in the ground. They were worn through use and polished by their passage. It had taken years for some to make the journey, sometimes more than a generation. The biographies of these and other items tracked paths across different regimes of value. Although some were to remain on these sites as a function of other rites, many were probably exchanged at these times, passed on and out into different local systems. Pottery was also moved, the tempers in non-local clays reflecting links between people that were often extensive. Vessels were brought to use in the giving of food, the majority better suited to consumption rather than storage. Once they had fulfilled that role, they became midden or offering. Because they revealed the hands of those who had made them, pots brought relations into focus at these moments.

Stone and clay are durable. They survive for us to recover and this can lead us to overestimate their importance. In all probability, they are just the tip of the iceberg, the last trace of networks that saw animals, people and even ideas move from one line to another. Although some were what we choose to call exotic, many were more local in origin, reflecting the scale at which relations were most often addressed. What was important was that their passage was mediated through the liminal conditions established at enclosures. These were places at which different regimes of value overlapped. There it was possible to suspend some of the usual conventions of reciprocity and to give added weight to particular transactions. The potentials offered by prestation could be contained. Watched over by the spirits of the past and by the assembled company, these were pivotal moments.

When the time and the audience was right, monuments that stood for the collective became arenas for competition and display. Not only that, the episodic quality of enclosure use sustained a sense of duration in gift giving. Convention dictated that debts and returns could only be met at these places and times, and this meant that relations would persist between gatherings. Certain exchanges made it possible for elders or lineage heads to accrue symbolic capital. This could be drawn upon for help in building or clearing, in fighting or for other purposes. Sometimes it was simply the authority to speak and act in other rites that was gained, but this could be challenged at another round and was just one of the levels at which transactions were made. Each had consequences for the ways that relations within and between communities would settle after dispersal.

Before that happened, there were rituals of closure, perhaps more deposits and the levelling of ground. While some sites were left open, others saw the earth restored, circuits marked by lines of posts. Restoration and departure marked a return to the familiar order of things. As kin left with stock, some enclosures were abandoned altogether. Others saw a rump remain, a line who stayed nearby and sometimes in the interior. The pattern varied from site to site and from one year to another. Kin went back to their valleys and slopes of the season. With them went the pattern of events they had witnessed and the detail of those in which they had played a part. Some carried relics, limbs bound together for burial at tombs or for interment elsewhere. Some carried themselves in a different way, a reflection of their inclusion in new companies. One in the company of elders; one of the women or one of the men; one who was tied to other lines. With them too were new animals and tools, perhaps cloth and even new kin. Each carried a different link and a particular acknowledgement to those who had scattered along different paths.

12 The pattern of things

They came back every afternoon with bundles of sticks, backs bent beneath hides that held the brush together. That was the way at these times. While men and women spoke of things they had yet to learn, the young were set to gathering for the fires. It took half a day, each morning taking them a little further from the circle. Windfalls grew thin on the ground.

The children were content with the task. They knew that the fires were kept high at these times, not even dwindling while the company slept. If they fell at night, souls would wander from the place and lose their bearings. Their bones had just been lifted and cleaned, and it was important that they knew which path to take. They had to wait until the living dispersed. Only then could they follow the embers that were carried back to scattered lodges for the winter. They had been told this many times, so often that it now seemed they had always known. That was how things were. It was as much a fact as the bodies of brothers or sisters laid to rest in the ditches that defined the circle. They often heard them calling just before the dawn.

The children knew something else as well. Long fires at night meant a break from the usual pattern of things, something extra in the stories they heard and in the flow of events around them. Beyond the danger and the drama, there was gossip and more casual intrigue. All had to be absorbed, stored for use in the long nights that approached.

The days had passed and now were gathered into two full hands: ten days of exchange and negotiation; ten nights in the company of ghosts. At first, the children had stared at each other, wary of kin whose names were not their own. Names spoken rarely, or in anger at their fires, faces they did not see when they closed their eyes. Things had been different the last time some of them had come. Then it had been only close kin, hearthsharers making offerings for the renewal of their line. This time the circle had been wider. The children had huddled as they put face to name and name in turn to story. Catching some of the potency of events, they mapped the ties between their lines in the pattern of their playing.

That had been ten days before. Since then, the gathering of windfalls had melted the ice between them just as surely as the spirits had brought the forest to life with their breath. When the elders spoke of the blood and other ties that bound them, they grafted each truth on the frame of these casual affinities. Most faces had become familiar. They would be remembered when the circle was broken, looked for when it joined again, or when paths were crossed. In time, some of them would marry. Some, perhaps, would fight.

Freed from their gathering, the children turned their attention to the cattle they had helped to tend on the way. Most remained hobbled on the edge of the clearing, but five had fallen beneath the axe. There was sport to be had in poking at the carcasses as they jerked on the ground. Dragging at the blood with their sticks, they pulled it into trails. It clung to the grass like an old man's spittle, growing thicker as it cooled, first brown, then black against the green. They argued over who would eat the most before scattering from a curse for straying under busy feet. Pulling back and out of the way, they watched as practised hands took the animals apart. Breastbones cracked beneath well-placed blows and hides seemed to come away of their own accord. The heads and first cuts were removed and put to one side for the dead. They would take part in the feast that night and without the gift might turn their backs upon the living. Their portions would be placed in the ditches with other gifts.

Tonight was important. The day had seen a marriage between two of the strongest lines, witnessed at the river which made one arc of the circle. At the place where the old ones had stepped ashore and where the dead had once been returned to the water, they had watched as customary exchanges were made. Gifts and words had been powerful. There had been boasts that all would grow fat before the night was done. Before the sun had set, all would gather again. Moving from the edges of the clearing, they would cross the line. They would take their places at the fires and eat, adding to the songs and following the dances. It would be dawn before the last head felt the earth.

Within talk of what would happen, most knew that the night was also important because it was almost the last. A few of the lines would soon be turning gravel and other debris back into their ditches before leaving. Those with the longer journeys and those who were anxious to return to lodges near the hills. They were always the first to feel the bite, and there was much to be done before the cold shrank everything. Most trades had been concluded, and there was agreement among many on rights of access. Spring would see new calves and help with new ventures, confirmation of bonds that had been recognised in the circle. With help and good fortune, there would be no conflict when the land was reborn.

The old ones watched. They had made the pattern many times and looked on as it was formed again. Each time it seemed that a new element was added, a twist in the tale. It was never repeated exactly. Few names had changed since the circle was drawn. Yet the threads that ran out across the land traced a picture that would not remain still. Some herds grew while others weakened. A year could see thin calves turn fat. There was always a chance that the pattern would be lost. That was why they watched. The dead held the circle together and everything else in its place.

Windmill Hill.

Melbourn.

Briar Hill.

Hambledon Hill.

Figure 54

13 Changes in the land

Monuments are often fundamental to the persistence and direction of social memory, yet many possess a quality that at first glance seems contradictory. Recruited by the living, they can change in form and in significance. They can bolster ideas or positions far removed from those which held sway at their first construction. They can even become a focus for competing visions of the order of things. At the same time, they retain a sense of the timeless and the eternal. The assertion of new values often goes hand in hand with an evocation of continuity, of an unbroken line between present and past. That capacity can be lost and it is always open to question, but it can be regained when traditions are invented to create a line where none existed before.

This quality is crucial for our understanding of how earlier Neolithic enclosures developed over time. One of the initial purposes that many served was the provision of a common cultural focus within nature. Their use was pivotal to the recognition of bonds between people. As a routine part of the seasonal round, scattered families brought their stock to rich pastures or woodland clearings, by rivers or on hills, and lived for a time in the company of others. Within and around these arenas, it was possible to renew a sense of the collective, to mediate conflicts between lineages and confirm distinctions within groups. Artefacts, ideas, animals and people circulated between lines as consequences of these moments and, more often than not, these practices drew upon the past, the past of earlier generations and the past of ancestral time. People assembled and sought the renewal of the world through exchange, through dealings with their dead and with the world beyond.

This was a pattern repeated many times. Intervals varied and there were occasions when only a few assembled for local observance, but the rhetoric of re-enactment was strong. The world needed to be made again and new currents would bring scattered lines together. As they had from the outset, many enclosures persisted as the focus of collectives. Embedded in cycles of movement, they grounded the renewal of that collective in the past and in the other cycles of life. Through these times, they made the landscape possible and brought the distant into people's lives. The return showed respect for the past and for the traditions that bound the collective. Strengthened by the cleaning and redigging of ditches or the clearing back of scrub, revelation came with excavation. Then, as now, it threw up traces to be interpreted. Old kin and old gatherings, remnants of the past in the present.

Tradition was powerful but it was not a dead hand. Like exchange, returns reformed as much as they renewed, even when they drew legitimacy from the past and from repetition. An amalgam of invention and forgetting shifted the boundaries and the meanings of many enclosures over time. Traditions were reworked so that the values invested in these places could be drawn upon for different ends. These changes were often gradual and unremarkable, resulting at times in piecemeal patterns of use or abandonment. Other sites saw more consistent reworking, new features and changes in both the character and the scale of boundaries. Histories grew in different ways from the original idea. That these changes were sometimes contentious is suggested by one of the more dramatic tableaux uncovered at Hambledon Hill. Here the skeleton of a young man was found near the earthworks of the Stepleton enclosure, face down and buried beneath a meagre covering of chalk. He had been shot in the back, perhaps while running, falling as the flint tore into his flesh. The tangle of bones revealed that his fall had trapped the small child he had been carrying; a child smothered by the body that had sought in vain to offer protection.

There is a pattern beyond the violence of this moment. Hambledon Hill was just one of several enclosures where long and varied histories culminated in attack and destruction. This was far from the norm, but it is perhaps the most vivid demonstration of a change in the place of enclosures in the political geographies of the time.

Figure 55 Body in ditch at Hambledon Hill, Dorset. (Photo: Roger Mercer.)

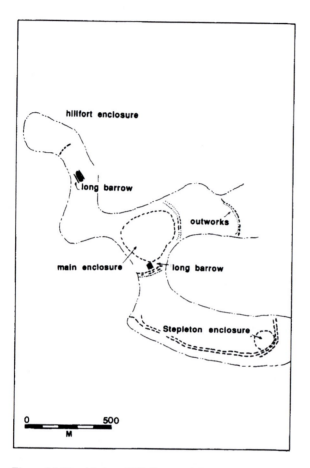

Figure 56 Hambledon Hill, Dorset (after Mercer 1988).

Reworking monuments

Reworking took many forms, gradual and alluvial in some places, dramatic and abrupt in others. Locally and regionally varied, these patterns were more than a simple reflection of broader changes in the configuration of social landscapes. They lay at the heart of social and political life as it unfolded from one generation to the next. In the dispersed conditions inhabited by earlier Neolithic communities, questions of tenure, ancestry and authority were addressed in equally dispersed and varied ways. But crucial values cohered around enclosures and this made them powerful instruments of change.

Details vary from one site to another. Despite their respect for an inner core, the addition of concentric circuits within one or two lifespans, and occasionally over centuries, marked more than the passing of time. It was a reiteration of traditional values. At Orsett, Whitehawk, Briar Hill and others, additional ditches also created more complex arenas of value. Space became more graded and at times this gave expression to hierarchies through the containment and choreography of people. Where passage was a function of kinship or initiation, more distinctions could be drawn between individuals or even different lines. While local rites could still be focussed on elements within each circuit, the whole carried the potential for broader divisions. Original circuits were also respected in a rather different way. At Fornham All Saints, a second enclosure was cut in relatively close proximity to the first, close enough for the two monuments to be regarded as paired. Here again it is difficult to determine whether there was an interval between these acts of construction. However, it is likely that this pairing is a function of sequence. This may also explain the proximity of Rybury and Knap Hill, which lie within an hour's walk of each other on the same chalk ridge. Recent aerial reconaissance also suggests a pattern of pairing enclosures on the lower-lying ground of the Thames Valley.

Similar developments may account for a second enclosure close to Etton. Known as Etton Woodgate, the site lacked many of the complex features and deposits seen on its neighbour, but earlier Neolithic flintwork and clusters of pits in and around the site suggest a measure of contemporaneity. Why this should have happened remains unclear. The answer may be prosaic. At Etton, for example, it may be that waterlogging led to the abandonment of one circuit and its reinstatement close by. However, this is not easy to demonstrate and we should allow that other factors played a part. There may have been differences in the significance accorded to each circuit, distinct rites and activities undertaken within their bounds. It may also be that the shift reflects a change in the fortunes of different lines. Proximity brought a reference to tradition, but there was also a break with the past, a chance to manipulate the frame in which important events took place. A new enclosure was free from the baggage of memory and historical association with particular kin groups. It offered a new start in cycles of social negotiation. Perhaps there were even times when an old enclosure simply became bad ground. Where crops failed widely or when disease and even conflict took stock and people, a new circuit offered the chance of a fresh arena in which to seek the renewal of the social and natural world. The recurrent pattern of paired enclosures in parts of the Thames Valley suggests that, here at least, replacement rather than reiteration became accepted practice.

A more common development than the pairing of enclosures was the consolidation of perimeters, the reworking of ditches or the addition of palisades. At Haddenham, excavation has revealed a sequence that finds echoes on many sites. Larger than its fen-edge counterparts at Etton or Great Wilbraham, the Haddenham enclosure lies on the Upper Delphs, a peninsula of gravel surrounded by more low-lying basins. Sitting at three metres above sea level, the single circuit of ditch segments cut into a matrix of gravels, sands and clays. Unlike its neighbours, the site has little evidence of occupation. Death and exchange were prominent here. Founded as a chain of irregular pits, reworking saw the boundary assume a more consistent circuit of longer ditches and fewer causeways. Here, as elsewhere, important thresholds were flanked by skull fragments, non-local artefacts and hearth or food residues. Patterns of localised recutting are evident in specific ditches and there is no evidence for any bank. The line was reinforced instead by the raising of a substantial timber palisade. Gardom's Edge also saw changes. Here certain causeways were blocked some time after the boundary was established, piles of gritstone boulders making more continuous lengths of bank.

The boundaries of other enclosures saw yet more dramatic developments. At Whitehawk, Hambledon Hill and Abingdon, causeways are absent from the outer ditches, creating a more continuous line. Palisades and fencing were also added, just as they were at Orsett, Hembury and Hambledon Hill. This parallels the appearance of continuous ditch circuits around a number of contemporary tombs. There is a more definitive sense of closure in these cases, a clearer and more explicit line being drawn. Crickley Hill exemplifies many of these trends. Here the passage of time saw one, then two lines of ditches cut off an elevated promontory on the Cotswold edge. Hollows and banks were consolidated in places by drystone walling and there is evidence for fenced pathways into an interior rich in traces of occupation and other activities. Settled during later phases but also a focus for ceremonial, the ditches, banks and palisades were reworked over many generations becoming ever more complex with time.

These breaks with tradition may be read in several ways, but they imply a shift of emphasis, from ditch as threshold, to ditch as categoric boundary. Here were lines where crossing was impeded and more effectively controlled. And where earlier circuits had embodied the collective, if segmented, character of labour, these more continuous lines cut through those distinctions. They no longer stood as metaphors for the constitution of the broader social group. Perhaps labour itself was organised by more singular directions.

It may be no coincidence that these developments were often most marked where enclosures developed a clearer association with settlement over time. Rectangular buildings were constructed at Crickley Hill and there are ditch deposits consistent with midden. At Abingdon, the space between inner and outer ditch saw occupation, residence within the fabric of the monument itself. This trend finds an oblique parallel at Hambledon. Here there are differences between the Stepleton enclosure and the larger circuit crowning the centre of the great chalk hill. Both were contained within extensive outworks, massive timber ramparts and banks which ran for several thousand metres, boundaries clearly visible from the vale which fell away to the south and west. Developed some time after its neighbour, this smaller enclosure had a closer association with settlement. Burials and fragments of human bone are present, suggesting an interweaving of the living and the dead, but internal features and more local assemblages suggest a more consistent presence.

Elevated above the surrounding land, people lived in close proximity to an arena associated with the dead of many generations.

Sometimes reworking involved the creation of a different monument altogether. There are a number of sites where long or oval mounds were added to existing earthworks. At Barrow Hills, the mound containing two articulated bodies was raised in close proximity to the Abingdon enclosure. This was a pattern repeated at Knap Hill, where Adam's Grave stands out on the skyline. Climbing from the Vale of Pewsey, the barrow draws the attention and it is just as prominent when looking west from the enclosure itself. Perhaps it was meant to be viewed in this way, the sun highlighting the profile of the mound as it set. Oval or round barrows have also been recognised at Maiden Castle, Robin Hood's Ball, Roughton and Whitesheet Hill. In each case, proximity to the enclosure may have been an important concern. At Hambledon Hill, the association between the main enclosure and a barrow was more direct and was strengthened by close parallels in the structure of their respective ditch deposits. The new monument was woven into the fabric of the old.

There were also cursus monuments. These have been recognised at several enclosures, parallel lines bisecting the circuits at sites like Etton and Hastings Hill. These would have been dramatic additions when freshly cut. At Fornham All Saints, a cursus cut across the pair, a direct line between two points. Massive linear mounds were also constructed at Maiden Castle and perhaps at Crickley Hill. These 'bank barrows' took the long mound tradition to its logical conclusion and inscribed a new form on the existing earthworks.

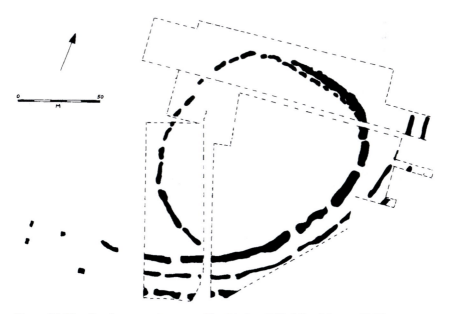

Figure 57 The Stepleton enclosure at Hambledon Hill (after Mercer 1988).

Once these were established, it was no longer possible to regard or move across the hill in the same way.

How should we understand these changes? Like settlement, new monuments were imposed as purposive and calculated acts, but what purposes did they serve? One possibility is that each, in its own way, was a strategy through which the associations and roles of older enclosures could be reconfigured. Inscribed by gatherings over many generations, these were the focal points for events that reproduced the order of the social landscape. Ancestral rites and the transformation of the dead joined the present to the past and ghosts watched over the crossing of other thresholds: initiation, marriage, dealings with others, relations mediated by various exchanges. To assert a measure of control over these places was to appropriate the events themselves, to create the conditions in which they might be worked to a sectional advantage.

The significance of certain practices was also changing. Exchange had always been central to the renewal of relations and to competition between groups. This latter role increased in importance with time. Tournaments of value within certain enclosures became a more strategic and assertive form of diplomacy. Inflicting debts through gift giving brought prestige and renown and this had consequences long after people had scattered. This may help to explain changes in the distribution of stone axes from distant sources. These expanded as the earlier Neolithic progressed, although movement remained hand to hand. Although it had always been important, fascination with the distant gave an added weight to exotic artefacts, and this in turn added to their use in more competitive bouts of gift giving. Brought into focus when people came together, these changes were recognised most clearly at enclosures. Perhaps it was because they also carried a sense of the distant with them that axes had sometimes to be buried at enclosures. It was here that they had once moved into local regimes of value. Death brought a renegotiation of

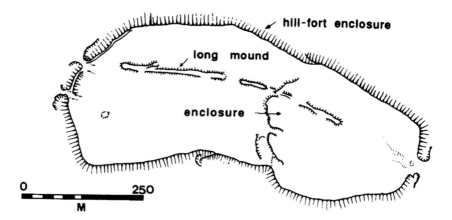

Figure 58 Maiden Castle, Dorset, showing the position of the long mound in relation to the enclosure.

more distant ties of affiliation and this may have been marked by the burial of important tokens where people once met.

The pursuit of sectional interests was manifest in many ways. Built close at hand or on the perimeter of an enclosure, barrows inserted new people into the stories and associations of the place. At a time when tombs became more closely linked with the dead from specific lines, the burial of individuals under ostentatious mounds asserted a claim to the enclosure and all that it stood for. Bank barrows served similar purposes, although their scale suggests that labour itself became a medium through which people could demonstrate authority. Perhaps this was another of the reasons why segmented ditches were no longer so important at certain sites. With a concerted focus on ancestors and sometimes on celestial alignments, the building of cursus monuments involved a more radical departure from tradition. Although they rose just the same from collective labour, they heralded a new order to the pattern and perhaps the significance of traditional ancestral rites. History was still important and that was why these new alignments cut into earlier features. Imposition gained a certain legitimacy where there was a reference to the past. But events now turned in a different way and this may have initially been to the advantage of some rather than others. There were new possibilities for inclusion and exclusion, new forms of knowledge and ideas to which only some could have access.

Occupation achieved similar ends by different means. Perhaps it was a privilege asserted by only certain lines. Where this was the case, residence brought with it the exclusion of others and an expression of a greater affinity with the powers of the place. Settlement did not mark the end of ceremonial events. Instead, it involved a shift in the extent to which particular lines placed themselves between enclosures and the broader corporate group. It created new conditions for access and for participation in important events. Those who lived within old perimeters demonstrated their proximity to the past and through this it was possible to exert a more determinate influence on proceedings. Perhaps the consolidation of boundaries was a strengthening of the line that separated people. Here the loss of segmentary ditches was a demonstration of the unity of those who dwelt within. Massive timbers and areas of freshly cleared ground spoke of more opposed relations with those who stood outside. At places like Offham, where human remains were concentrated in the outer ditch, perhaps the dead of close kin added greater definition to that line.

We cannot always tell what the outcomes of these varied strategies may have been. At a few sites, however, the result was sudden and dramatic. Along with Hambledon Hill, Hembury and Carn Brea saw attack and destruction, violent death and the toppling of burning palisades. Crickley Hill was also attacked. Burnt hurdles and rubble were pushed into ditches, perhaps as buildings blazed and people scattered. The pink and altered limestone still bears witness to the intensity of the fires. Some screens also had arrows embedded in their fabric and there are clusters of arrowheads around

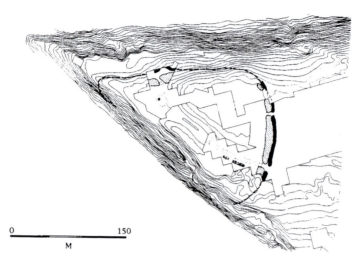

Figure 59 Crickley Hill, Gloucestershire: Phase 1d (after Dixon 1988).

important entrances reflecting fighting focussed on these points. Although they were well suited to defence from archers, the last boundaries at the site proved insufficient to the task.

What seems to have been at issue at these times was something even more profound than the death of people. It was the death or transformation of the place, the removal of boundaries and dwellings and all they had come to represent. At Hambledon, the burning was so intense that the oak timbers of the outworks burnt below as well as above ground – a hallmark of concerted destruction. Conflagration was followed by the collapse of charred wood and the pushing of scorched chalk into ditches. It was beneath this rubble that bodies were found during excavation. Some may have been buried quickly, but others had already fallen prey to birds, dogs and wolves before a covering of chalk removed them from sight. There is little evidence to suggest the reconstitution of old circuits after these attacks.

Changes in the land

In creating a focus for the collective and in concentrating important rites and events, enclosures established conditions that could be worked to selective advantage. Exchange, marriage and ancestral rites offered the potential to consolidate or challenge the accepted order of authorities among the living. While the rhetoric of events spoke of the ties that bound, outcomes could be influenced to serve the interests of some rather than all. There may have been little that was new in all this. Regional politics had always had a fluid quality, particularly as one generation gave way to another. But, with the passage of time, the pursuit of certain interests involved a more dramatic

Figure 60 Distribution of arrowheads around one of the entrances at Crickley Hill, Gloucestershire (after Dixon 1988).

reworking of the past at enclosures and this had consequences for broader social geographies.

Geographies were changing in other ways as well. Equally gradual and alluvial, the landscapes of routine experience were reconfigured from one generation to the next. Subsistence remained extensive and varied in its roll-call, the patchwork of wood and open ground just as dynamic. However, genealogies continued to grow and there are hints that both the scale and the character of routine movement slowly changed as the period progressed. Stoneworking traditions were reworked, taking a turn away from the consistent use of good stone to make portable, flexible tools. Major quarries continued to be visited and there was an increase in the range of tools that people made in many areas. Many of these served as tokens of identity and value but, in general, core working reflects a more varied and even more profligate use of stone. It is as if people were often more content to use whatever lay to hand for various tasks. Surface scatters also vary. Many seem to cover larger areas than their predecessors, as if settlements were sustained over longer periods or re-established at closer intervals. These trends are difficult to understand and they resolved themselves over centuries, but they suggest a consolidation of the ranges over which many communities lived and worked. Pathways became deeper, pastures and arable more persistent over time.

There were other changes too. As generations passed, many tombs became more monumental. Though this was sometimes a cumulative process, often it was more dramatic and concerted, suggesting a greater or different weight behind the values tombs embodied. The trend towards individual burials implies a more explicit concern with the genealogies and aspirations of particular families. Where many tombs had once bound communities together, now they drew attention to the eminence of particular lines and the biographies of certain people. The past of these places now focussed on specific individuals. These changes probably arose for a variety of reasons, many of them quite local in their extent. Like the continued use of older tombs, the raising of long or oval mounds showed respect for the past and for the accepted way of doing things. However, these places were more actively recruited in the face of tensions and conflicts of interest: friction between elders and young adults, competition between the elders of different lineages and perhaps the heads of specific lines. Questions of access to land, resources and labour may have sometimes set the spark to these developments, but often it was the political capital of the past and the ancestors that was at issue.

Given their drama and abrupt finality, it is tempting to tie up talk of these changes with the acts of destruction seen at sites like Crickley. However, the evidence actually pulls us in different ways. Warfare may have been endemic, but only a few enclosures were attacked; there was no singular outcome to arguments over authority and tenure in different areas. Long after the fires had died at Hambledon, some enclosures continued to provide a foundation for signal events. Processing along the cursus at Etton or gathered along the mound at Maiden Castle, people stood on land with a powerful history and this contributed to the weight they attached to proceedings. At others, respect was acknowledged more tacitly. At Haddenham and Windmill Hill, deposits in the upper fills of certain ditches represent activities that postdated the currency of each monument. How far these took the form of persistent open settlements or shorter episodes remains uncertain but, in both these cases, it was not considered essential to revive the entire monument from its dormant state.

In many regions, old enclosures were simply abandoned, losing some of their prominence as landmarks. No longer cleaned or maintained, the lines and contents of old ditches were still remembered and perhaps even venerated. Passing with stock, close kin probably hung the stories that they told to their children on the frame of surviving earthworks. A few even sought to renew their ties with the past through acts of local commemoration. However, respect and the renewal of the social world no longer turned upon the reconstitution of the monuments themselves.

What do these developments signify? One response might be to take the falling away of enclosures as evidence of a lack of concern for the themes that once animated their use. This seems tempting, but there is a wealth of evidence to the contrary. In many regions, people continued to recognise themselves as parts of broader collectives, realising ties through congregation, celebration and exchange. But these themes now turned around other places and other practices: cursus monuments, burials and the henges and stone circles that we class as later Neolithic.

Few of these developments involved an abrupt or total break with the past. References to the distant and the remote seem to have grown in importance, as did the burial of individuals in many areas. Yet new places and practices also grew out of a process of reworking local traditions. As before, those traditions varied as did the scale and longevity of individual monuments or complexes. Those who built and congregated at later arenas often did so with one eye on the histories and genealogies of specific hilltops or valley sides. The past remained an important focus, as did the world of the supernatural. Varied in the significance that they held for contemporary communities, events along the Dorset cursus gained some of their weight from references made to ancient houses of the dead. Established while Hambledon was still remembered a day's walk to the west, this line across the rolling chalk defined a break with traditional patterns of herding and residence. At Long Meg and her Daughters, the stones of the impressive circle seem to overlie an older enclosure and it is difficult to see this as anything other than a deliberate reference. Communities had always gathered here, kin from neighbouring valleys and those from beyond the high, open country to the east. When people assembled in and around the perimeter, attention switched back and forth between the broader landscape and the antiquity of half-remembered celebrations on the hill. In much the same way, those near the henge and circles at Avebury would have been able to raise their eyes westwards to where an older gathering place lay draped across Windmill Hill. Avenues directing people to and from the henge worked with the topography to create views of older monuments that spoke of particular lines. Whether old enclosures were still prominent in oral tradition at these times is difficult to determine. Some were no more than a poorly remembered heritage. Stories of others were still populated by specific people and events, but both confirmed a long tradition behind gatherings in new perimeters.

The idea of enclosure was also reworked to rather different ends. Henges and stone circles suggest a continued concern with the demarcation of specific places and times at which important collective events could be anticipated. Many henges are situated on important lines of access and communication – rivers or gaps that gave access across higher ground. Nowhere is this clearer than in Cumbria, where both circles and henges were often situated at the confluence of valleys or near important breaks in

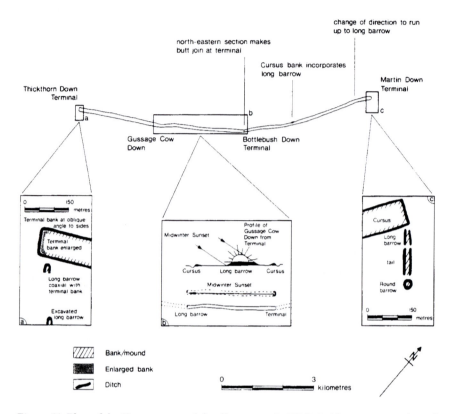

Figure 61 Plan of the Dorset cursus (after Barrett *et al.* 1991). Laid out in a number of stages, the cursus appears to have served as a boundary between areas devoted to the dead and those parts of the landscape in which we find more evidence for settlement. Incorporating earlier tombs into its fabric, and aligned on the midwinter sunset, the monument remained a focus for funerary rites and periodic gatherings for many generations.

the Pennines. As they had in earlier times, these places drew a line between arenas of value, at the same time encouraging gatherings by their location. Where present, astronomical alignments confirmed that periodic assemblies and life cycles were in step with a more basic cosmological order.

With internal ditches, more massive banks and fewer entrances, henges took the sense of demarcation even further than before. Not only that, there is little evidence for the shifting pattern of occupation and formal events that many older sites had witnessed. Here it seems that a more rigid boundary separated ritual from the everyday. Although people assembled on the margins at certain times, convention provided an effective barrier to residence within many henges. Reworking the idea to different ends, competing lines sought to maintain an exclusive character to the tournaments of value that took place within henges. Many gathered and laboured and, through this, a sense of a wider federation was periodically renewed. The public celebration of a broad collective was still central, particularly in Wessex. But there were times when only a few could enter: the initiated, or those of a certain affiliation or standing in the region. Particular lines, particular people; different companies at different scales. Unless they stood on the banks themselves, those on the margins could neither enter nor see what unfolded within these lines. Monuments that bound the land together could still be used to selective advantage.

We can see an expression of this process at Stonehenge. Here the chaotic variety of phases and episodes that make up the sequence began with a small enclosure that echoed older monuments in its form. A close parallel can be found at Flagstones in Dorset. The circle was recruited in many ways, episodes of intense activity set within more quotidian encounters. As before, there were times when small companies assembled, women, men, or a particular line. People still passed while herding, finding the earthworks empty of others. However, this was also a place of initiation and of gatherings, a place to honour the dead, a place to engage in exchange and competition with others. The perimeter was reworked and many timbers were added,

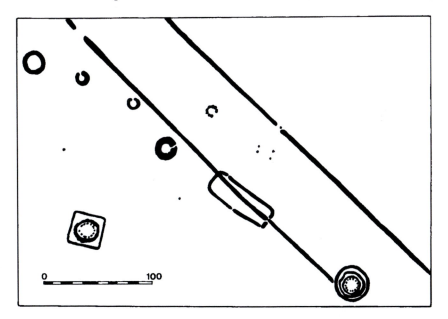

Figure 62 Detail of the monument complex at Dorchester-on-Thames, Oxfordshire. Here an earlier Neolithic mortuary enclosure was cut/augmented by a larger cursus monument. The passage of time saw the addition of ring-ditches and henges to this complex and the use of the area for gatherings, processions and funerary rites. While the earliest components of the complex are aligned on important lunar events, the sun appears to have been the main point of reference for the builders and users of the later sites.

circles, facades and avenues suggesting processions and a growing emphasis on hidden rites. When the stones were erected to mimic timbers, authority may have been conferred on those who saw the sun rise along the avenue and over the heel stone at Midsummer. More durable than timber, the stones, like the ancestors, would persist for all time. A sense of endurance added weight to the values that people worked into the place. With time, the monument also became a focus for the burial grounds of different lines. The proximity of the dead suggested a genealogical depth to the ties that bound certain people to the place and all that it represented. Those who could sustain that link could work the ties between earth and sky in their interests.

Stonehenge was just one site among many. Similar concerns were addressed at many later Neolithic monuments, although the history of events varies from one area and generation to the next. Different regions saw people draw in different ways upon common themes. At Knowlton in Dorset, several henges were built in close proximity, perhaps a sequence of new arenas rather than the elaboration of an older circuit. Complexes also developed in areas such as the Millfield Basin and in Cumbria. In the Peak District, we also find broadly contemporary monuments that operated at different scales. Arbor Low was established near to older barrows. Cut into the limestone, this dramatic henge with now recumbent stones was itself a focus for later burial. This was also a place of gathering and display, of tournaments of value and varied calendrical rites. The scale of the monument speaks of extensive ties between communities. A day or two's walk to the east, the moors of the Peak District saw very different scales of congregation. Those who moved and worked across the moors may have visited Arbor Low at certain times but, increasingly, they also addressed more local concerns through the ring cairns and circles they established in the uplands. These were places of more limited

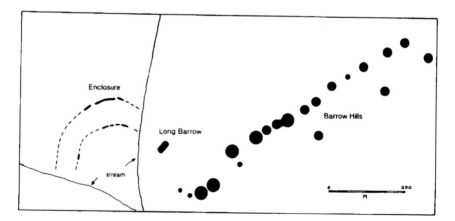

Figure 63 Abingdon, Oxfordshire. Situated between two watercourses, the enclosure at Abingdon remained a point of reference for later activity. Many generations after the long barrow was constructed, the area saw the development of a later Neolithic and Early Bronze Age barrow cemetery.

observance, some visited seasonally by only a handful of families. Anchors and points of reference for the dead. Over time, these circles became the focus for persistent settlements. Cairnfields suggest a long fallow, even seasonal occupation of land that still shifted and turned between open ground and woodland. By this time, the old enclosure on Gardom's Edge had been eroded from memory. Whatever ghosts attended the place, they could not prevent the use of the bank as a simple dump for stone from neighbouring plots.

The forgetting of Gardom's Edge echoes the fading of many early enclosures from social memory. Though they often persisted as earthworks or low stone lines, many lost their names and their prominence in the social landscape. Banks and ditches were absorbed back into the earth. While some were settled or were passed by later generations of herders and hunters, they were no longer drawn upon in dealings with the dead or with others. Addressed elsewhere and to different ends, the shifting of those concerns consigned enclosures to a past that became more nebulous and remote with time. A mother acknowledged the place in passing; it still held the ghosts of her line. Her grandson caught a more vague outline, a place still waved at in stories of before. His grandaughter saw open country, a slope where people bent to turn the earth by hand.

AFTERWORD

This book has taken us along a number of different paths. It has attempted to trace the conditions in which the idea of enclosure was taken up by communities of the early fourth millennium. It has explored how routine traditions were both a context for enclosures and important in their own right for the definition of the social world. And, it has tried to follow the ways in which the idea of enclosure was reworked over time. As such, it is a work of synthesis and this brings with it certain problems. Where narratives tack back and forth between the general and the particular, it is easy for local and specific histories to get lost within the flow of a grander process. In this sense, to talk of an idea of enclosure in the singular may be to miss the varied understandings that people had at the time. This is to some extent inevitable; we will never capture these times and places in their entirety, and certainly not in a singular account. Even if we could be transported back in time to enter an enclosure and speak to informants, it would still be impossible. However, the traditions that can be traced in our evidence do seem to indicate the recognition of common themes, even if these were worked to varied ends.

Why people should have drawn upon the idea of enclosure at this time is still a question that remains open. What I have suggested here is that there were a variety of reasons, conditions that were both geographically and historically specific. In a climate of ideas sustained by extensive networks of contact and communication, changes in the character and trajectory of land use certainly played their part. They raised a series of concerns for the fertility of the land and of people, and new ways of thinking about the relationship between present and past. At the same time, patterns of living associated with having herds and tending crops brought with them changes in how people understood their ties to land and their relations with others. Dispersed though the landscape was, the passage of time saw a consolidation and sedimentation of those ties. There were other themes too, ones which cannot be reduced to simple consequences of subsistence change. The negotiation of local renown and the satisfaction of conflicts of interest were also crucial; social and political relations between groups were both volatile and malleable. Beyond all else, the idea of enclosure provided a frame through which it was possible for communities to recognise and negotiate their place in broader social geographies.

Once established, these arenas for the celebration of the collective established new possibilities for social action. Where identity, position and customary rights of access were tied to ancestral rites and to exchange, the concentration of these practices in a single place and time afforded new potentials for the pursuit of sectional interests. In one sense at least, the creation of many of these monuments established the foundations for new forms of political authority. Other themes continued to be of importance for those who gathered and laboured around enclosures. More localised senses of kinship, affiliation and progression remained crucial, addressed in the particular details of feasts, rites of passage and moments of formal deposition. They were also present when small groups passed or camped in close proximity to these powerful places. To talk, as some have done, of a mixing of 'the rational and the irrational' may be to set up an artificial divide, one that may not have been recognised at the time. However, it does go some way towards catching the tangle of values that bound routine and ritual together at enclosures. By the later Neolithic, many of the elements in this tangle had been dispersed across several distinct categories of ceremonial monument. Clearer lines were drawn between different areas of social experience. Rough circles themselves became more geometric.

We could end the line here were it not for the pattern at Hambledon Hill with which this book began. In a few cases, certain enclosures were rediscovered. More or less forgotten, they were set within invented traditions that sought legitimacy in a distant and malleable past. Nowhere is this clearer than at the Trundle in Sussex, where survey has revealed a complex of earthworks from both the Neolithic and the Iron Age. Excavated by Cecil Curwen, the circuits of the earlier enclosure lie within the hill-fort of the later period. There is a strong sense of symmetry between the two monuments. This is not unique – several hill-forts were imposed on older enclosures. The simple fact of elevation encouraged this pattern. However, at the Trundle, as at Maiden Castle and Hambledon, the plan suggests a stronger purpose. The builders of the later boundaries took inspiration from the layout of a monument that was already ancient to the order of more than eighty or a hundred generations.

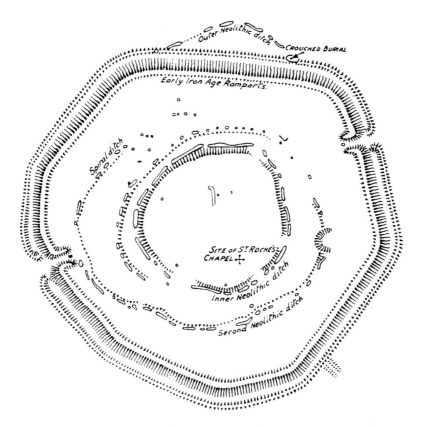

Figure 64 The Trundle, Sussex (after Curwen 1934).

How far memory had blurred into myth or oblivion by this time we shall never know: the boundary between real and fictive genealogies is difficult to draw. What is clear is that in the very different landscapes of the Iron Age, the values ascribed to new banks and ditches gained a permanence and gravity from a past remembered and respected anew.

14 Post excavation

The two riders climbed the side of the hill, the ground changing beneath their horses as they went. The night had been cold, and as the sun rose across their backs, they dawdled so the warmth had time to penetrate. The early light was split by the copper and iron in their stirrups. Leaving the arable behind, they rode past scrub and rough grazing, across lynchets that marked the line of long-forgotten fields. They did not notice.

Reaching the crest, the riders pulled to a stop and dismounted. They rolled their saddles down and bound the hooves to hinder straying. The horses heads dropped, sniffing at the cords and at the ground around them. Indifferent. Forgetting their burdens, they turned their attention to the pasture that still thrived outside the line. The two riders turned and walked up to the entrance. Framed by great white banks and massive timbers, the gatehouse seemed to hang above them, its porch a flurry of activity as they approached. Again, they did not notice. Their thoughts were on the digging.

The work had begun the year before. Then, the idea had been clear. The crops had been poor for a third summer and pools of stock were low. The land had turned its back upon the living and many, in their turn, set themselves against their neighbours. Boundaries were more tightly drawn. Each month, it seemed, there was news of local disputes and sporadic fighting; weapons had been cleaned and sharpened for the first time in years. There had even been deaths along the line and demands for reparation. There was also talk of changes far to the east and across the great water, rumours which circulated like distant thunder when elders met and talked. All seemed at odds.

The heads of all the strongest lines had decided upon the enclosure. In this they had the agreement of their shamen. It would be a return to the old ways, to the time of the first heroes. They would set a place apart and, in that place, all who were of their blood could come in safety. There the tribe could trade and settle their disputes, hold tournaments and set store for the leaner seasons. It would be the pivot for their wheel. Each line would contribute, working every summer in the cutting of chalk and the raising of banks. For many, it would be an obligation, but what did that matter when it was for the good of all? The rhetoric was strong or hollow, depending where you stood.

There was only one hill on which the enclosure could stand. Always the last to lose the sun each evening, the tallest rise set itself apart. Besides, they had all heard the stories about who was buried on the crest. Some said it was a chief dressed in gold, others that an entire clan lay frozen beneath the turf. Still more said it was haunted by the last of the old shamen. Those watching flocks had for many years whisperered that the largest mound was the outline of a buried shield, the longest the shoulder of a giant ox. The banks that could still be seen at dusk would set the pattern for their work.

The brothers had returned in step with the agreement. Reaching the compound where their kin were quartered, they answered casual greetings and removed their cloaks. Squatting by the fire, they exchanged news with the others, catching up on what had happened in the ten days since they had gone to follow their ploughs. Within minutes, the talk submerged into the low muttering that was common when knives were out. There was nothing new. Some were still playing less than their part in the labour. A few had presumed to stand above the work, mustering others on their behalf. One day, things would be different.

By mid-afternoon they were working with the others. As a few called instructions from the lip of the ditch, most cut and dug, piling the spoil into baskets that were carried to the top of the new bank. It was hard going. Pulled in different ways by the plough, their bodies took time to remember the customary shapes and moves of digging. Soon, however, they were back into the rhythm of it, matching baskets with others who had not been away. The iron made light work of the chalk. Only rarely did axes or wedges fasten so tightly that they needed a kick to jerk them loose. The digging absorbed them. In no time they were as white as all the rest, the slick of clay and chalk made more fluid by their sweat. Exposed in the ditch fills, wet flint caught the light like polished iron.

The pattern would have gone unchanged till sunset had it not been for a cry from above. Cutting back turf further in from the bank, one of the boys had discovered a dark circle in the chalk. A vivid contrast to the rock, it was about the same width as a small cartwheel. It was not the first, and the finding of a pit always sent a charge through those who dug. Putting down their picks, the brothers climbed and huddled with some fifteen men and women to see what would emerge.

The boy crouched forward. Apprenticed to the smiths who worked at the far end of the hill, he seemed less concerned than the others. That was not surprising. Those who worked metal were always a little apart from the rest. His hands seemed to sense what lay beneath. Using a thin blade, he followed the edge of the circle, scooping the rich, black earth into his other hand. Aware of the eyes that peered over his shoulder, he wondered how he would hide copper or gold if it was found. His hands moved quickly, and he hunched his shoulders to obscure the view. It was not long before his blade hit something hard. He felt it but the others heard. Resigning himself to the loss of a prize, he quickened in the digging. Earth was scattered to his side as bets were made on what would appear.

They had not expected the skull. Pottery perhaps, or one of those strange stone ploughshares. A skull was altogether different. The dark orbits stared up and past the onlookers. The jaws were clenched in an expression impossible to read. The gaze caught their eyes so strongly that no one noticed the thin flint blade lying just to one side. It would not have mattered anyway; the earth was stuffed with such pieces.

So the stories were true. Perhaps they had been wrong to doubt the elders after all. Here was proof that there were people beneath the turf. Some said the skull was a trophy, laid at the edge of the great chief's grave as a mark of respect. Others were not so sure. Hesitant to touch the bone, they wondered if it was an offering of a different kind, a token from the times when it was said the shamen had practised powerful magic. A few scoffed at the idea, recalling the shepherd lost on the hill many years before. Perhaps someone with a grudge had surprised him while he tended the flock. No one was certain, but it was enough to bring the day to a close. They would have to talk before digging continued. If the ghosts of the dead were to honour their labour, it would not do to show them disrespect.

Postscript

Barbara Bender and Mark Edmonds

B: So – first – why are we talking to each other? If you remember, Routledge asked me to write a preface extolling (!) your approach and discussing some of the ideas that informed the writing. But I thought it'd be much more interesting to have a conversation – and not just about the theory but the many different layerings within the book. What did you think about using this sort of communication?

M: I thought it was an excellent idea for a number of reasons. First, it does create an opportunity to talk about some of the ideas and issues that have informed the writing. At the same time, I think it mirrors the way in which many of my ideas have developed over the past few years in conversation with you and with others – in other words, through dialogue. There's no question that these conversations have had a big impact on the way that the book has turned out.

B: I think that there are a whole series of issues that it would be good to get into: about the structure and content of the book; the use of stories; questions about illustrations, and so on. But, first, I would like to say something about why I think the book is exciting and innovative.

Quite a number of archaeologists have begun to write about embodied landscapes – within Britain alone there's John Barrett, Chris Tilley, Julian Thomas, Richard Bradley, Colin Richards, myself, and more besides – but I don't think any of us have really found a way of talking about prehistoric people as people who are intimately knowledgeable about natural resources, who confidently exploit their environment, who move around, and visit, and exchange, and feud. And that's what you've focussed on: groups of people aggregating and dispersing, moving with the seasons. And what you hammer home – and this is the big difference between your approach and earlier environmental archaeology – is that these people, whatever they're doing, whether it's the most mundane activity or the most formal, are always working within their understandings, within the knowledge passed down from generation to generation. Doing things the right way. You call the book *Ancestral Geographies*, and that's such a good title – it's about a lived landscape that's filled with the voices and wisdom of those that have gone before. What you emphasise is that it doesn't matter whether you're clearing a patch of ground, or opening a pit to extract flint, or burying the dead, or coming together at one of the enclosures, the same ritualised – and varied – understanding of the world permeates each and every action. You're quietly demolishing the divide created by most archaeologists between ritual and everyday landscapes.

And, of course, you're also explaining how, as they go about their daily concerns, they not only reproduce the social order, but also negotiate and subtly, often unknowingly, change it.

Your turn: why did you want to write this kind of book?

M: I guess it is a response to a number of things. It's my response to the archaeological evidence, as I understand it, for the earlier part of the Neolithic in southern Britain. It's also, though, a response to other people's writings. Archaeologists that you've just mentioned, who are grappling with issues relating to how we build an understanding of past social life and past social change. Of course I've drawn on their ideas, and found them positive and useful. But at the same time, this book is also an attempt to deal with a series of problems that I found in a lot of their work. I felt that they often missed the ways in which particular places and times were inhabited, and how those patterns of occupation were implicated in the understandings that people had of themselves and the world around them. A lot of the archaeological accounts just seem unnecessarily abstracted: they miss the very points that they're attempting to address. As I said in the book, it seems like we've often ended up with very thin descriptions of both the archaeological evidence and of the people who created or lived through that evidence.

B: I know, from having talked with you before, that, originally, the book was going to be rather different. It was going to focus much more on enclosures and less on routine life. Then you had the burglaries, and as a result – after the tears and whisky – you decided to open up the book to look at a wider range of places and activities. I think that shift of emphasis was very important. If you had just kept the focus on enclosures, you wouldn't have been able to create that sense of movement back and forth between the everyday and the more special or performative moments.

M: Yes, definitely. In its original format, the book was more concerned with a specific archaeological category – causewayed enclosures. Most of the discussion of routine experience, which has ended up being so important, was no more than a 'background' chapter. In a way, the original format was led by the category, rather than by the contexts or situations of those monuments. With hindsight, I recognise that I was uncomfortable with that category-driven approach. What the rewrite has allowed me to do is place much more of an emphasis on the threads that run back and forth between different tasks, places and times. It's also given me the chance to try to get beyond the unhelpful dichotomy that opposes routine and ritual experience. If you remember, that was something that we tried to get at in the paper we wrote a few years ago, a page or so of which has ended up in chapter one.

B: I want to ask you some questions about theoretical issues. It's very clear that you're pulling in a lot of theoretical insights in this book, and yet you don't very often step back and talk about the ideas or their sources. That may be why there's a tempo to the chapters that, to be honest, I found slightly reiterative. You start each of the main chapters by invoking a particular place – maybe Wayland's Smithy or Knap Hill – you focus on some aspect of that place, and then open up into a more generalised discussion of forest clearance, or flint working, or whatever. There's a certain sonority which sort of works – it becomes almost a mantra, a repetition, whereby the reader comes to understand the way in which all activities are imbued with people's under-standings of each other and of the world around them. Sure, you do break up the main text by using stories, but you could have also broken it, or opened it up, by ruminating on the ideas and arguments that have stimulated and excited you. What made you decide not to?

M: Well, I guess one of the things that I wanted to avoid was the common tendency to start out with twenty or thirty pages of abstracted discussion on theoretical issues, followed by a separate discussion of material. I wanted to make the ideas more thoroughly embedded in my treatment of the material. That is one of the reasons why the book has the structure that it does. You're right – I wanted to create a tempo that would help carry the idea that many aspects of people's lives have a reiterative quality. I guess that the other thing I wanted to avoid was using theoretical discussion as a form of rhetoric.

B: What does that mean?

M: Talking and arguing about ideas is absolutely central to what we do. But there are occasions when you can't help thinking that theoretical discussions are recruited to lend an authority to particular statements about the past, irrespective of whether the theory really elucidates the material evidence.

B: It is true that the theory does often seem to float free of the evidence. Still, I think you could have embedded more discussion of ideas that have influ-enced you, and your responses to those ideas.

M: I suppose I was worried about the flow of the book, and it is an experiment. I wanted to write a less 'academic' book – hence the lack of footnotes. But yes, it might have been useful. There are lots of debts. In both the content and the structure of the book, Bourdieu has definitely been a big influence, as have Raymond Williams and John Berger. I guess Bourdieu's concept of habitus comes closest to capturing how even the most basic aspects of people's lives are caught up in social reproduction. As he puts it some-where, understanding is often written in the body, and that's something that Marcel Mauss also acknowledged quite beautifully in his work on how we learn various practical techniques. Much of that learning is tacit and embo-died and it carries with it other values and ideas.

Of course, Bourdieu writes extensively and in the abstract about his particular theory of practice. But what I find most stimulating is when he begins to work on particular ethnographies, on particular people and places and times, when the ideas and arguments are thoroughly worked into the discussion. The conditions that people act upon and their agency comes through without having to be highlighted or signposted, and that's important because so much operates at the level of the taken-for-granted. I wanted to see if I could acknowledge this by working in a similar way. There's nothing particularly new in much of this. It's the path taken by Chris Tilley in *Phenomenology of Landscape* and by John Barrett in *Fragments*. I think both books encourage ways of thinking about how past material traditions were inhabited. But again, both stop short of exploring the tangle of acts and relations bound up in routine practice – it all ends up being far too neat!

I'll tell you some of the other people whose ways of thinking and writing inspired (and daunted) me. People like E. P. Thompson and *Annales* historians like Bloch, Le Goff and Ginzburg. Again, what I admire is their ability to take specific moments, places or events and unravel them; exploring relations, identities and historical conditions in complex but utterly compelling ways. Ultimately, they are all remarkably good writers and it shows!

B: That's a good hit-list! I guess they're all 'history in a grain of sand' people. They understand that the smallest detail of a life works within numerous, ever-enlarging, contexts. The blur between micro- and macro-scale is something that concerns you, isn't it? You're determined, throughout the book, to get a sense of how change is piecemeal and localised and accidental. Flux and process. But the difficulty is moving between scales - showing how small, historically contingent, processes build into long term, quite fundamental, changes in social relations.

M: Yes, I agree. And I think that for 'time' you can also read 'space', because I think we have a similar problem with geographic scale. Whether you're going to talk about things that operate at the level of continental Europe – which is what publishers always like – or about the islands of Britain, or about specific regions. Moving backwards and forwards between those scales is very tricky but essential.

Think back to a lot of the social evolutionary and structural marxist models of the last twenty or so years. One of the criticisms levelled at them was that they were overly systemic. They didn't really provide a satisfactory account of how the social structures that were being discussed were created, sustained and changed over time. There was no sense of agency or history. Barrett is very good on this in *Fragments*. Part of the problem was the chronological scale at which explanations were pitched. They dealt with vast tracts of time and it was hard to see how these histories of structures could be connected to the rich variety of material traditions that were worked and reworked from one generation to the next. Nor, of course, did they deal with that sense of variability that one encounters when one moves between valley systems, between regions, and certainly across the continent. There are patterns and trends that we can see at various scales. The challenge is trying to grasp how they articulate. How did a family of cattle herders living in what is now the Fens inhabit a broader climate of contacts and ideas? What interested me was how the processes that we identify and study were carried forward in local and historically contingent ways. In other words, how was order possible at all and how might it have been understood at the human scale?

B: There is a fine passage in your book where you catch a sense of how scales of space elide. People from different places are coming together at an enclosure: 'The geography of a larger area could be mapped in this space between the trees'.

Returning again to aspects of theory. There's another issue that you touch on, but only briefly: the way in which interpretations change through time. There's a short discussion in one of the enclosure chapters, and another when you're talking about the Mesolithic/Neolithic transition. Why didn't you make more of this?

M: There could have been a lot more on the history of interpretation. I find it absolutely fascinating. In the end though, I decided to keep it brief. What I wanted to try and get across was that very few things that we say about the Neolithic and certainly about enclosures are actually 'given'. The period name has meant and continues to mean different things to different people. And it's the same with enclosures. Once we step beyond talking about the actual shape and size of ditches, what we feel these places are about, why they were created, how they were used, how they developed over time, are things that are constantly open to reassessment. Sometimes this is because of new evidence, but it's also because the world in which we write about the past is far from static. Archaeological orthodoxies change and there are always differences of opinion.

B: I guess it would be fair to say that your explanatory framework represents a thread within current orthodoxies! One which questions the earlier tendency to offer an explanation of a phenomenon, one that celebrates variability, that opts for multiple, messy explanations – the 'sometimes it was this, sometimes it was that, sometimes it was lots of things' approach. The emphasis on multiple usage parallels the contemporary emphasis on multivocality.

M: We love to create categories. Chris Evans talks about this in an excellent article on enclosures that he wrote in 1988. He talks about the problem of 'top down' explanations – how we identify a category, give it some sort of strength as an archaeological phenomenon, and then attempt to find a single explanation for why this particular category appeared. What this fails to allow for is the possibility that, while things might be inspired by a broad set of similar ideas, the way they're taken up, the way they develop, is incredibly varied. So you end up with a curious paradox: the category you're working with has such blurred edges that it may not actually be useful to think of it as a single category at all!

B: The chapter on enclosures, where you talk about changing interpretations, also contains one of the few discussions in the book on continental affinities. Why doesn't the question of continental connections come up in other contexts? Isn't that avoidance also part of an unspoken dialogue that you're having with earlier, or indeed current, explanations of change?

M: I could have talked more about continental backgrounds earlier on. But with enclosures, I felt it was important to situate some of the history of interpretation in relation to broader arguments about cross-channel relations and questions of colonisation versus indigenous development. I wanted to suggest that these issues could be looked at differently. We don't have to choose between wholesale colonisation or developments in 'splendid isolation'. It may well be more useful to envisage a relatively free flow of people, artefacts, animals and ideas going backwards and forwards across the channel. Maybe it's us that make the channel into a barrier, not them, and that flow can't be captured in a single term like colonisation.

B: I don't disagree with you, but I do think that, again, our desire to focus on local identity, local variability, is a rather particular contemporary preoccupation. Pretty soon we'll have to embark on broader discussions of connections between places and people, movement and exchanges of different sorts. A confusion of degrees and forms of connectedness.

M: Sure. Just so long as we don't simply swap one scale of explanation for another, instead of thinking about their articulation. What I'd hoped I'd got a little closer to was the idea that although we might be dealing with what we call small-scale societies, we were also dealing with people with extensive social geographies. The scale of those geographies was partly to do with how far they moved on a regular basis. But it was also a function of their location within webs of exchange relations and oral traditions that probably tacked back and forth between the immediate and the distant. We have no difficulty in envisaging those networks going across the Pennines. Why not the channel?

B: The question of different scales also permeates the structure of the book. There are the 'main' chapters, and then, operating at a different scale, there are the stories. I liked them. The bits I liked best were when people were doing things: making flint tools, sharpening wooden stakes. I felt that in those vignettes on working practices your own experience really shone through, and marked out one of the big differences between your approach and that of people who – like myself – have a theoretical but not a practical understanding. But aside from those vignettes the important thing about the stories was that they allowed you to be imaginative without provoking a counterblast from the more traditional 'stick with the facts' brigade. The scenes are evocative and they rework the materials presented in the main chapters. I wonder, though, whether you found it a struggle – like, how far were you prepared to go beyond 'the known' in recreating a sense of particular place and time?

M: I guess the idea of combining different forms of narrative was inspired by the work of two people, John Berger in particular, but also Raymond Williams. There's the close attention to labour I suppose, and perhaps the idea of juxtaposing different narrative forms to come at something from several directions. I've always found this very powerful with Berger, whether it's in his own work or in his collaborations with Jean Mohr, in books like *A Seventh Man*. I think that experimenting with different forms of writing is essential if we want to capture the mess, complexity and intimacy of the processes and the people that we're interested in. Just look at the contrast between the subtle vocabularies that we use to evoke a sense of how overtly performative rituals work in people's lives, as opposed to the impoverished language that we use to talk about the bulk of more routine experiences. The stories are an attempt to enrich that language, by recreating a sense of intimate moments, even gestures, that are, nonetheless, caught up in the broader flow of things.

I was also trying to do other things with the stories. For example, I wanted to give a sense of immediacy to the conditions that might have created a specific form of evidence – the moment when a flake detaches from a polished stone axe, or when wood resists your best intentions.

B: Yes, those were good moments. But you did hold back, didn't you, from evoking a more detailed sense of how people thought about their world?

M: That's true. They're not completely open. There are no names and, apart from the first story, I've held back on fleshing out the content of particular myths or the details of cosmologies. I did this because I accept that these are things that we'll simply never be able to capture from the archaeological evidence and I wanted to leave a space to acknowledge the gap. It's interesting, because in the longer story that I'm now working on I haven't held back. Here though, I felt that it was appropriate for things to be a little more circumscribed.

B: There's a strong sense that the stories, and also the longer chapters, are informed by ethnography. How do you feel about using ethnographic analogies?

M: I've tried to avoid taking anything 'off the peg', so to speak, and I acknowledge the very real problems that have arisen and continue to arise when ethnographic presents are imposed upon the past. I think though, that there are various forms of broad generalisation that we can make. We've already talked about the idea that cultural understanding is something that is embodied and lived through in all aspects of one's practice. We can follow that idea through in thick descriptions of the material traditions that we trace. There are also ideas about the complex senses of identity and community that people can sustain, and how those can be woven into what Tim Ingold calls the 'taskscape' and into 'talk'. To this you could add general arguments about relations between people and things, and about exchange. And of course there is the importance of the past itself. Irrespective of the location or content of particular ethnographies, the past is often a powerful weight and a resource, immanent in many aspects of people's lives.

B: Another thing I liked about the stories was your thoughtful, but not pushy, gendering of activities – the way you avoided many of the stereotypes about who does what. You have women knapping flint, age grades performing different tasks and so on.

M: Some of the gendering is meant to be provocative and challenge-taken-for-granteds, others are meant to pass almost unnoticed. What I did want to

get across though was how the 'chain of operations' that make up many tasks would have linked people and perhaps involved the movement of tools and knowledge between people. What I definitely wanted to avoid was simply creating a 'past-u-like' – a romanticised, 'weren't they wonderful' sort of past.
B: One last thing: the illustrations. Your stories sit rather oddly against many of the illustrations that you use. You've tried to make the text very accessible, but the illustrations, particularly the plans, are more conventional and are, by definition, 'coded' – you need prior knowledge in order to understand them.
M: You're right, and it's partly a product of the fact that I came to the images far too late. I fell into the trap of seeing the illustrations as appendages to, rather than implicated in, the text. The plans are the worst. They give schematic 'bird's eye' views that in no way capture how a place was set in the land, or how it was approached, or how it worked at a human scale. I did experiment with photo-collages and with writing on photos, and though I think these have lots of potential, I wasn't very happy with them. 'Reconstruction' drawings are difficult, particularly if, like me, you can't draw people very well. If you're going to work with someone else then, again, you have to start the process early on. I guess that this time I've experimented more with the words. Next time it might be better to work on the images first.

Bibliography

Although I have not used in-text references, a variety of books and articles have been crucial in preparing this work. In what follows, I have tried to reflect the thematic, material and site-specific reading that I found valuable. This is by no means an exhaustive list, but it should provide a way into many of the issues discussed here. At the time of writing, a volume with a wealth of new survey data for enclosures is also being prepared by the Royal Commission on the Historic Monuments of England. Readers are encouraged to consult the RCHME volume for more detailed plans and information on the location of enclosures.

Appadurai, A. (1986) *The Social Life of Things: Commodities in Cultural Perspective*. Cambridge and New York: Cambridge University Press.

Ashbee, P. (1965) 'Wayland's Smithy', *Antiquity* 39: 126–33.

Ashbee, P. (1984) *The Earthen Long Barrow in Britain*, Norwich: Geo Books.

Avery, M. (1982) 'The Neolithic causewayed enclosure, Abingdon', in Case, H. J. and Whittle, A. W. R. (eds) *Settlement Patterns in the Oxford Region: Excavations at the Abingdon Causewayed Enclosure and Other Sites*, 10–50. Council for British Archaeology Research Report 44. London.

Bamford, H. (1985) *Excavations at Briar Hill*. Northampton: Northampton Development Corporation.

Barker, G. and Webley, D. (1978) 'Causewayed camps and earlier Neolithic economies in central southern England', *Proceedings of the Prehistoric Society* 44: 161–85.

Barnatt, J. (1996) 'Moving beyond the monuments: paths and people in the Neolithic landscapes of the Peak District', *Northern Archaeology* vol. 13.

Barrett, J. (1994) *Fragments from Antiquity*. Oxford: Blackwells.

Barrett, J. C. and Kinnes, I. A. (eds) (1988) *The Archaeology of Context in the Neolithic and Bronze Age: Recent Trends*. Dept of Archaeology and Prehistory, University of Sheffield.

Barrett, J., Bradley, R. and Green, M. (1991) *Landscape Monuments and Society: The Prehistory of Cranborne Chase*. Cambridge: Cambridge University Press.

Basso, K. (1984) 'Stalking with stories: names, places and moral narratives among the western Apache', in Bruner, E. (ed.) *Text, Play and Story*. Illinois: Waveland Press.

Bedwin, O. (1981) 'Excavations at the Neolithic enclosure on Bury Hill, Houghton, W. Sussex, 1979', *Proceedings of the Prehistoric Society* 47: 69–86.

Bedwin, O. (1982) 'Excavations at Halnaker Hill, Boxgrove, West Sussex', *Bulletin of the Institute of Archaeology, University of London* 19: 92–5.

Bedwin, O. (1983) 'Excavations at Halnaker Hill, Boxgrove, West Sussex (second season)', *Bulletin of the Institute of Archaeology, University of London* 20: 80–3.

Bedwin, O. (1984) 'The excavations of a small hilltop enclosure on Court Hill, Singleton, West Sussex, 1982', *Sussex Archaeological Collections* 122: 13–22.

Bender, B. (1978) 'Gatherer-hunter to farmer: a social perspective', *World Archaeology* 10: 204–22.

Bender, B. (1993) *Landscape Politics and Perspectives*. Oxford: Berg.

Bloch, M. (1989) *Ritual, History and Power*. LSE Monographs on Social Anthropology 58. London: Athlone Press.

Bloch, M. and Parry, J. (eds) (1982) *Death and the Regeneration of Life*. Cambridge: Cambridge University Press.

Bourdieu, P. (1977) *Outline of a Theory of Practice*. Cambridge: Cambridge University Press.

Bourdieu, P. (1984) *Distinction: A Social Critique of the Judgement of Taste*. Cambridge: Cambridge University Press.

Bradley, R. (1984) *The Social Foundations of Prehistoric Britain*. London: Longmans.

Bradley, R. (1987) 'Time regained: the creation of continuity', *Journal of the British Archaeological Association* cxl: 1–17.

Bradley, R. (1990) *The Passage of Arms*. Cambridge: Cambridge University Press.

Bradley, R. (1993) *Altering the Earth*. Society of Antiquaries of Scotland Monograph 8. Edinburgh.

Bradley, R. (1998) *The Significance of Monuments*. London: Routledge.

Bradley, R. and Edmonds, M. (1993) *Interpreting the Axe Trade*. Cambridge: Cambridge University Press.

Bradley, R. J. and Gardiner, J. (eds) (1984) *Neolithic Studies: A Review of Some Current Research*. British Archaeological Reports (Brit. Series) 133.

Care, V. (1979) 'The production and distribution of Mesolithic axes in Southern England', *Proceedings of the Prehistoric Society* 45: 93–102.

Care, V. (1982) 'The collection and distribution of lithic raw materials during the Mesolithic and Neolithic periods in southern Britain', *Oxford Jnl Arch.* 1.3: 269–85.

Case, H. and Whittle, A. (eds) (1982) *Settlement Patterns in the Oxford Region*. Council for British Archaeology Research Report 44. London.

Casimir, M. J. (1992) 'The dimensions of territoriality: an introduction', in Casimier, M. J. and Rao, A. (eds) *Mobility and Territoriality. Social and Spatial Boundaries among Foragers, Fishers, Pastoralists and Peripatetics*. Oxford: Berg.

Connah, G. (1965) 'Excavations at Knap Hill, Alton Priors, 1961', *Wiltshire Archaeological Magazine* 60: 1–23.

Connerton, P. (1989) *How Societies Remember*. Cambridge: Cambridge University Press.

Cosgrove, D. (1983) *Social Formation and Symbolic Landscape*. London: Croom Helm.

Crawford, O. G. S. (1937) 'Causeway settlements', *Antiquity* XI: 210–12.

Crawford, O. G. S. and Keiller, A. (1928) *Wessex from the Air*. Oxford: Clarendon Press.

Cronon, W. J. (1983) *Changes in the Land: Indians, Colonists and the Ecology of New England*. New York: Hill & Wang.

Cunnington, M. E. (1912) 'Knap Hill Camp', *Wiltshire Archaeological Magazine* 37: 42–65.

Curwen, E. (1930) 'Excavations in the Trundle', *Sussex Archaeological Collections* 72: 100–30.

Curwen, E. (1934) 'Excavations in Whitehawk camp, Brighton', *Sussex Archaeological Collections* 77: 66–92.

Curwen, E. (1936) 'Excavations in Whitehawk Camp, Brighton, third season', *Sussex Archaeological Collections* 77: 60–92.

Darvill, T. C. (1981) 'Excavations at the Peak Camp, Cowley: an interim note', *Glevensis* 15: 52–6.

de Certeau, M. (1984) *The Practice of Everyday Life*. Berkeley: University of California Press.

Dixon, P. (1988) 'The Neolithic settlements on Crickley Hill', in Burgess, C., Topping, P., Mordant, C. and Maddison, M. (eds) *Enclosures and Defences in the Neolithic of Western Europe*, 75–8. British Archaelogical Reports (Int. Series) 403. Oxford.

Drewett, P. (1977) 'The excavation of a Neolithic causewayed enclosure on Offham Hill, East Sussex, 1976', *Proceedings of the Prehistoric Society* 43: 201–42.

Drewett, P. (ed.) (1978) *Archaeology in Sussex to AD 1500*. Council for British Archaeology Research Report 29. London.

Douglas, M. (1966) *Purity and Danger*. London: Routledge & Kegan Paul.

Edmonds, M. (1995) *Stone Tools and Society*. London: Batsford.

Eliade, M. (1954) *The Myth of the Eternal Return*. London: Routledge & Kegan Paul.

Entwistle, R. and Grant, A. (1989) 'The evidence for cereal cultivation and animal husbandry in the southern British Neolithic and Bronze Age', in Miles, A., Williams, D. and Gardiner, N. (eds) *The Beginnings of Agriculture*, 203–15. British Archaeological Reports 496. Oxford.

Evans, C. (1988a) 'Monuments and analogy: the interpretation of causewayed enclosures', in Burgess, C., Topping, P., Mordant, C. and Maddison, M. (eds) *Enclosures and Defences in the Neolithic of Western Europe*, 47–74. British Archaelogical Reports (Int. Series) 403. Oxford.

Evans, C. (1988b) 'Acts of enclosure: a consideration of concentrically organised causewayed enclosures 85–97', in Barrett, J. C. and Kinnes, I. A. (eds) *The Archaeology of Context in the Neolithic and Bronze Age: Recent Trends*, 65–79. Dept of Archaeology and Prehistory, University of Sheffield.

Evans, C. (1988c) 'Excavations at Haddenham, Cambridgeshire, a planned causewayed enclosure and its regional affinities', in Barrett, J. C. and Kinnes, I. A. (eds) *The Archaeology of Context in the Neolithic and Bronze Age Recent Trends*, 127–49. Dept of Archaeology and Prehistory, University of Sheffield.

Evans, J. G., Rouse, A. J. and Sharples, N. (1988) 'The landscape setting of causewayed camps: recent work on the Maiden Castle enclosure', in Barrett, J. C. and Kinnes, I. A. (eds) *The Archaeology of Context in the Neolithic and Bronze Age: Recent Trends*, 73–84. Dept of Archaeology and Prehistory, University of Sheffield.

Gell, A. (1985) 'How to read a map: remarks on the practical logic of navigation', *Man* 20.2: 271–86.

Godelier, M. (1985) *The Material and the Mental*. Cambridge: Cambridge University Press.

Goody, J. (1976) *Production and Reproduction*. Cambridge: Cambridge University Press.

Gow, P. (1995) 'Land, people and power in Western Amazonia', in Hirsch, E. and O'Hanlon, M. (eds). *Between Space and Place: Landscape in Cultural Perspective*, 43–62. Oxford: Berg.

Gregory, C. A. (1982) *Gifts and Commodities*. Cambridge: Cambridge University Press.

Healey, E. and Robertson-Mackay, R. (1983) 'The lithic industries from Staines causewayed enclosure and their relationship to other earlier Neolithic industries in Southern Britain', *Lithics* 4: 1–27.

Hedges, J. and Buckley, D. (1978) 'Excavations at a causewayed enclosure, Orsett, Essex, 1975', *Proceedings of the Prehistoric Society* 44: 219–308.

Helms, M. (1988) *Ulysses' Sail*, Princeton, NJ: Princeton University Press.

Hobsbawm, E. and Ranger, T. (eds) (1983) *The Invention of Tradition*. Cambridge. Cambridge University Press.

Hodder, I. (1990) *The Domestication of Europe*. Oxford: Blackwell.

Holgate, R. (1988) *Neolithic Settlement of the Thames Basin*. British Archaeological Reports 194. Oxford.

Holgate, R. (1990) *Prehistoric Flint Mines*. Shire: Princes Risborough.

Ingold, T. (1982) *Hunters, Pastoralists and Ranchers*. Cambridge: Cambridge University Press.

Ingold, T. (1993) 'The temporality of landscape', *World Archaeology* 25(2): 152–74.

Kahn, M. (1990) 'Stone faced ancestors: the spatial anchoring of myth in Wamira, Papua New Guinea', *Ethnology* 29: 51–66.

Kendrick, T. D. and Hawkes, C. F. C. (1932) *Archaeology in England and Wales, 1914–1931*. London: HMSO.

Kinnes, I. A. (1992) *Non-Megalithic Long Barrows and Allied Structures in the British Neolithic*. British Museum Occasional Paper 52. London.

Kuchler, S. (1993) 'Landscape as memory: the mapping of process and its representation in a Melanesian Society', in Bender, B. (ed.) *Landscape Politics and Perspectives*, 85–106. Oxford: Berg.

McBryde, I. (1984) 'Kulin greenstone quarries: the social contexts of production and distribution for the Mount William site', *World Archaeology* 16: 267–85.

Madsen, T. (1988) 'Causewayed enclosures in southern Scandinavia', in Burgess, C., Topping, P., Mordant, C. and Maddison, M. (eds) *Enclosures and Defences in the Neolithic of Western Europe*, 301–37. British Archaeological Reports (Int. Series) 403. Oxford.

Manby, T. (1988) 'The Neolithic in eastern Yorkshire', in Manby, T. (ed.) *Archaeology in Eastern Yorkshire*, 35–88. Dept of Archaeology and Prehistory, University of Sheffield.

Mauss, M. (1936) 'Les techniques du corps', translated 1979 in *Sociology and Psychology: Essays of Marcel Mauss*. London: Routledge & Kegan Paul.

Mauss, M. (1954) *The Gift*. New York: Norton

Mercer, R. (1980) *Hambledon Hill – A Neolithic Landscape*. Edinburgh: Edinburgh University Press.

Mercer, R. (1981) 'Excavations at Carn Brea, a Neolithic fortified complex of the third millenium BC', *Cornish Arch.* 20: 1–204.

Mercer, R. (1988) 'Hambledon Hill, Dorset, England', in Burgess, C., Topping, P., Mordant, C. and Maddison, M. (eds) *Enclosures and Defences in the Neolithic of Western Europe*, 89–107. British Archaeological Reports (Int. Series) 403. Oxford.

Moffett, L., Robinson, M. A. and Straker, V. (1989) 'Cereals, fruit and nuts: charred plant remains from Neolithic sites in England and Wales and the Neolithic economy', in Miles, A., Williams, D. and Gardner, N. (eds) *The Beginnings of Agriculture*, 243–61. British Archaeological Reports 496. Oxford.

Moore, H. (1986) *Space, Text and Gender.* Cambridge: Cambridge University Press.

Morphy, H. (1995) 'Landscape and the reproduction of the ancestral past', in Hirsch, E. and O'Hanlon, M. (eds) *Between Space and Place: Landscape in Cultural Perspective*, 185–209. Oxford: Berg.

Musson, R. (1950) 'An excavation at Combe Hill Camp, Eastbourne, August 1949', *Sussex Archaeological Collections* 89: 105–15.

Palmer, R. (1976) 'Interrupted ditch enclosures in Britain: the use of aerial photography for comparative studies', *Proceedings of the Prehistoric Society* 52: 161–86.

Piggott, S. (1952) 'The Neolithic camp on Whitesheet Hill, Kilmington Parish', *Wiltshire Archaeological Magazine* 54: 404–10.

Piggott, S. (1954) *The Neolithic Cultures of the British Isles.* Cambridge: Cambridge University Press.

Pluciennik, M. (1998) 'Deconstructing "The Neolithic" in the Mesolithic–Neolithic transition', in Edmonds, M. and Richards, C. (eds) *Social Life and Social Change in the Neolithic of North West Europe.* Glasgow: Cruithne Press.

Pryor, F. (1983) 'Questions not answers: an interim report of excavations at Etton, near Maxey, Peterborough, 1982', *Northamptonshire Archaeology* 18: 3–6.

Pryor, F. (1988a) 'Earlier Neolithic organised landscapes and ceremonial in lowland Britain', in Barrett, J. C. and Kinnes, I. A. (eds) *The Archaeology of Context in the Neolithic and Bronze Age: Recent Trends*, 63–73. Dept of Archaeology and Prehistory, University of Sheffield.

Pryor, F. (1988b) 'Etton, near Maxey, Cambridgeshire: a causewayed enclosure on the Fen edge', in Burgess, C., Topping, P., Mordant, C. and Maddison, M. (eds) *Enclosures and Defences in the Neolithic of Western Europe*, 107–27. British Archaeological Reports (Int. Series) 403: Oxford.

Pryor, F., French, C. and Taylor, M. (1985) 'An interim report on excavations at Etton, Maxey, Cambridgeshire, 1982–1984', *Antiquaries Journal* 65: 275–311.

Renfrew, C. (1973) 'Monuments, mobilisation and social organisation in Neolithic Wessex', in Renfrew, C. (ed.) *The Explanation of Culture Change: Models in Prehistory*, 539–58. London: Duckworth.

Richards, J. (1990) *The Stonehenge Environs Project.* English Heritage Monograph. London.

Robertson-Mackay, R. (1987) 'Excavations at Staines, Middlesex', *Proceedings of the Prehistoric Society* 63: 1–147.

Shanks, M. and Tilley, C. (1982) 'Ideology, symbolic power and ritual communication: a reinterpretation of Neolithic mortuary practices', in Hodder, I. (ed.) *Symbolic and Structural Archaeology*, 129–54. Cambridge and New York: Cambridge University Press.

Sharples, N. (1989) *Recent Excavations at Maiden Castle, Dorset.* English Heritage Monograph. London.

Smith, I. F. (1965) *Windmill Hill and Avebury.* Oxford: Oxford University Press.

Smith, I. F. (1966) 'Windmill Hill and its implications', *Palaeohistoria* XII: 469–81.

Smith, I. F. (1971) 'Causewayed enclosures', in Simpson, D. D. A. (ed.) *Economy and Settlement in Neolithic and Early Bronze Age Britain and Europe*, 89–112. Leicester: Leicester University Press.

Soffe, G. and Clare, T. (1988) New evidence of ritual monuments at Long Meg and her daughters, Cumbria', *Antiquity* 62: 552–7.

St Joseph, K. (1964) 'Air reconnaissance: recent results, 2', *Antiquity* 38: 290–1.

Strathern, M. (1988) *The Gender of the Gift.* Cambridge: Cambridge University Press.

Tacon, P. (1991) 'The power of stone: symbolic aspects of stone use and tool development in Western Arnhem Land, Australia', *Antiquity* 65: 192–207.

Thomas, J. (1990) *Rethinking the Neolithic*. Cambridge: Cambridge University Press.

Thomas, J. S. and Whittle, A. W. R. (1986) 'Anatomy of a tomb – West Kennett revisited', *Ox. Jnl Arch.* 5: 129–56.

Thomas, K. D. (1982) 'Neolithic enclosures and woodland habitats on the south downs in Sussex, England', in Bell, M. and Limbrey, S. (eds) *Archaeological Aspects of Woodland Ecology*, 147–70. British Archaeological Reports 146. Oxford.

Tilley, C. (1994) *A Phenomenology of Landscape*. Oxford: Berg.

Tilley, C. (1996) *An Ethnography of the Neolithic*. Cambridge: Cambridge University Press.

Turner, V. W. (1967) *The Forest of Symbols*. Ithaca, NY: Cornell University Press.

Turner, V. W. (1969) *The Ritual Process: Structure and Anti-structure*. Ithaca, NY: Cornell University Press.

Weiner, A. (1992) *Inalienable Possessions*. Berkeley: University of California Press.

Wheeler, R. E. M. (1943) *Maiden Castle, Dorset*. Society of Antiquaries Research Report 12. London.

Whittle, A. W. R. (1977) *The Earlier Neolithic of Southern England and Its Continental Background*. British Achaeological Reports (Int. Series) 35. Oxford.

Whittle, A. W. R. (1988) 'Contexts, activities, events – aspects of Neolithic and Copper age enclosures in Central and Western Europe', in Burgess, C., Topping, P., Mordant, C. and Maddison, M. (eds) *Enclosures and Defences in the Neolithic of Western Europe*, 1–20. British Archaeological Reports (Int. Series) 403. Oxford.

Whittle, A. W. R. (1995) *Neolithic Europe: The Creation of New Worlds*. Cambridge: Cambridge University Press.

Wilson, D. R. (1975) 'Causewayed camps and interrupted ditch systems', *Antiquity* 49: 178–86.

Woodward, P. J. (1990) *The South Dorset Ridgeway. Survey and Excavations 1977–1984*. Dorset Natural History and Archaeology Monograph 8.

Zvelebil, M. (1998) 'What's in a name: the Mesolithic, the Neolithic and social change at the Mesolithic–Neolithic transition', in Edmonds, M. and Richards, C. (eds) *Social Life and Social Change in the Neolithic of North West Europe*. Glasgow: Cruithne Press.

Index

Page numbers in bold denote an illustration and/or caption

Abingdon (Oxfordshire) 83, 85, 89, 100, 121, 139, **148**; multiple circuits 113, 115; reworking of 138; and settlement 138
Adam's Grave (Wiltshire) 80, 139
adzes 39, 41
age grades 31, 42, 43, 47
ancestors: defining of relations with by axes 42; proximity to as expression of privilege 30, 63; relationship with land through 20–1, 26, 69; and stoneworking 48; and tombs 58–9, 61, 69
ancestral rites 60–3, 69, 73, 104–5, 119, 140, 141, 142
animals: burial of 124; identification with people 118; importance of livestock 26–7; movement of 27; woodland clearance and management of domesticated 23; *see also* cattle; stock husbandry
Arbor Low 148
arrowheads, leaf-shaped 18, 19, 39, 56
Ascott under Wychwood 60
Avebury 145
axes 19, **19**; burial of in enclosures 140–1; changes in distribution of stone 140; circulation 41, 42, 48, 128; defining of relations between people and ancestral world 42; deposition 42, 48, 123–4, **125**; production of 41, 46; as tokens of identity and value 39, 41, 42, 68

Barford 59
Barholm 85, **123**
Barkhale 83

Barrett, John 158
Barrow Hills **71**, 139
barrows 139, 141 *see also* long barrows
Beckhampton barrow 28
Beckhampton Road (Wiltshire) 61, **64**
beef 117
Berger, John 160
Blackpatch mine (Sussex) 36, **43**
blades 20, 38, 80
blood feuds 30
bones, human 123; bringing of to tombs to rest with earlier generations 60, 61; as circulated relics 59, 61, 70, 119, 120; dispersal 59, 61, 119; division of in tombs 63; and strengthening of links between communities 121
Bourdieu, P. 157–8
Briar Hill (Northamptonshire) 85, 88, **103**, 113, **133**; ditches 90, 102, 137; multiple circuits 84; stoneworking 114–15
Broadwell 93
Broome Heath (Norfolk) 18
burials 145; barrows and mounds 123, 141; of bones 60, 61, 63–4; and cattle 28, 64; in enclosures 119–20, 121–3; planting cultural remains 29; and skulls 119; trend towards individual 73, 121, 144; women and children 121–3; *see also* tombs
Bury Hill 85

Cairnfields 149
cairns 65, 71
Cambridgeshire fens 15, 17, 38
Cardington 85, 93

Carn Brea (Cornwall) 84, 85, 87, 89, 123, 141
Carrock Fell (Cumbria) 84, 87
cattle 68; burial of in tombs 28, 64; and enclosures 92; importance of 27–8; as source of standing 27–8, 118
causewayed enclosures 73, **86**, 110, 113–14
chiefdoms 99
children: burial of 121–3
Church Hill mine (Findon) **41**
Cissbury mine 36, **41**, **43**
Clare, John 3–4
Cleveland 59
Coombe Hill 83, **120**
cores 17–18, 20, 38, 80
Coupland (Northumberland) 92
Court Hill 85
Cranborne Chase (Dorset) 40, 70
Crickley Hill (Gloucestershire) 82, 83, 89; attack on 85, 141–2; construction of palisades 88; distribution of arrowheads **143**; land-use potentials around **91**; Phase 1b **102**; Phase 1d **142**; reworking of 138
Cumbria 145–6, 148
Cunnington, Maud 85
cursus monuments 73, 104–5, 139–40, 141, 145
Curwen, Cecil 83, 89, 150

Darion (Belgium) 95, **96**
dead 119–24; breaking up of bodies in enclosures 120; funerary ritual 119–21; making sense of death at heart of ways of thinking 7; passage of into ancestral realm 123–4; and tools 123–5; transformation of in enclosures 121; *see also* ancestral rites; burials
deer: clearance of woodlands as influence on movement of 23
defleshing 119, 120
deforestation *see* woodlands, clearance of
deposition 125; axes 42, 48, 123–4, **125**; and enclosures 115–17
Dorchester-on-Thames (Oxfordshire) 70, **147**
Dorset 27, 39–40
Dorset Cursus 40, 145, **146**
Dorstone Hill 86
Duggleby Howe (Yorkshire) **69**

enclosures 80–105, 110–29; abandonment of 135, 144–5; activities inside 114–15; attack on 135, 141–2, 144; breaking of bodies of the dead 120; building of barrows 139–40, 141; burials 119–20, 121–3; and circuits 83–4, 112, 113, 115; and the collective 101, 102–3, 134–5, 150; and constructing of society 98–103; construction and working on 99, 101–2; continental 93–8; cursus monuments as additions to 105, 139–40; and defense 85–6; deposition 115–17; ditches 90, 97, 101, 102, 103, 110; entry and crossing of thresholds 112–15; environs of 90–1, 92; and exchange 126–8; fading from social memory of early 149; and feasting 117–18; first building of 82; frequency and distribution 84–5; gatherings at 100–3, 111–12, 126; and hierarchies 95–6, 137; internal features 89–90; interpretation of 85; land-use potential around 91, **91**; pairing of 137; reasons for addition of new monuments to 140–1; reasons and purposes for 134, 149–50; relationship with LBK longhouses **94**, 95; and renewal of relations with the past 104; reworking and additions to 113, 135, 136–42, 145–9; and scatters 91–2; seasonal use of 92, 93, 100; settings and location 83, 86, 92, 99–100; settlement and occupation 85, 88–90, 91–2, 111–12, 138, 141; similarities between 83; and stock husbandry 92, 100; and stoneworking 114–15, 125, 126; topography 86–8; and transformation of the dead 121; *see also* individual sites
Etton (Cambridgeshire) 85, 88, **111**, 113, 115, **118**, 119, 139; circuits 83–4; deposition of axes 123–4, **125**; ditch deposits 110–11, **112**, 116–17, 125; ditches 90, 110; flooding of 93, 110
Etton Woodgate **111**, 137
Evans, Chris 99, 159
exchange 30, 81, 126–9, 135, 142, 145; centrality of to renewal of relations 126, 140; of exotic artefacts 128, 140; forms of transactions 127; gift giving 68, 127, 128, 140; and stone 39, 68

farming 16, 67
feasting 30, 64, 117–18, 127
fighting 30, 39

Five Wells chambered barrow
(Derbyshire) **66**
Flagstones (Dorset) 147–8
flakes 17, 18, 20, 38, 80
flint 15, 36, 38, 40, 45
flint knapping 16, 38, 46
flint mines 36, 44
food: as a gift 127; production of 16, 21,
23, 67; sharing 117–18
forests *see* woodlands
Fornham All Saints 84, 137, 139
France: enclosures 96–7
Freston 85
Fussell's Lodge 59, **60**, **62**, 65

Gardom's Edge (Derbyshire) 87–8, **88**,
102, 138, 149
gender categories 30–1, 42, 47
gift giving 68, 127, 128, 140
Godmanchester (Cambridgeshire) 105
grasslands 28, 29
Great Wilbraham **109**, **120**
Green Low chambered barrow **66**

Haddenham (Cambridgeshire) 65, **79**,
84, 101, 113, **114**, 117, 137–8, 144;
deposition of axes 123; mortuary
structures 59, **60**; reworking of 138
Halnaker Hill 85
Hambledon Hill (Dorset) 1–5, 9, 93,
116, 117, 123, **133**, **136**, 150;
association between enclosure and
barrow 139; attacks on 85, 141, 152;
causewayed ditch **90**; construction of
palisades 88; deposition **126**;
deposition of axes 124; features and
use of 3; land-use potential around **91**;
reworking of 138; and settlement 89;
skulls and bones found **116**, 119–20,
135, **135**; Stepleton enclosure **139**;
and stock husbandry 92
Hampton Lucy 85
Hanging Grimston 65
Hardy, Thomas 1
Harrow Hill mine 36, **41**, **43**, **45**
Hastings Hill 139
Hazard Hill 123
Hazelton long cairn (Gloucestershire) **74**
Helman Tor (Cornwall) 84
Hembury 83, 123, 138, 141
henges 145–8
Hetty Pegler's Tump 61
hierarchy 8; and enclosures 95–6, 137
High Peak 124

hill-forts 3, 85, 150
Hod Hill 3
hunting 16, 39

Icomb 101
Isleham 15

Kedington 91
Kendrick 83
Kilham 65
kinship 16, 30, 42, 73, 123; and
stoneworking 39; and tombs 62, 63,
64, 69
Knap Hill (Wiltshire) 80–1, **81**, **82**, 85,
91, 93, **109**, 121; Adam's Grave 80,
139; features 80, 82, 86–7; and
Rybury 84, 137
Knowlton (Dorset) 148

Lakeland fells: stone axe quarry **47**
landscape: changes in 67–74, 142–9;
reasons for change in 67–8; view of by
communities 20–1, 36
Langford 83
Langweiller 8, **94**, 95
Lanhill 63
LBK (Linearbandkeramik) 94–5, 96
livestock 26–7; *see also* stock husbandry
long barrows 40, 59, **66**, 123
Long Down mine **41**
Long Low bank barrow **66**
Long Meg and her Daughters (Cumbria)
86, 87, 145
long mounds 5, 6, 7, 65
longhouses 94–5, **96**
Longstone Moor **66**

Maiden Castle (Dorset) 83, 99;
association of long mound to
enclosure **140**; construction of linear
mounds 139–40; deposition of axes
123, 124; ditches **90**; land-use
potential around **91**; making of flint
axes **126**; skull in ditch **119**;
stoneworking 115
Mairy (Ardennes) 97
marriage 30, 81, 125, 127, 142
Mauss, Marcel 157
Melbourn 113, **118**, **133**
Menneville (France) 97
Mercer, Roger 119–20
Mesolithic 5, 19, 37, 42, 67–8
Michelsberg (France) 97
Millfield Basin 148

mines 41, **41**, 42–4, 45
Minninglow cairn 65, 66
monuments 4–10, 134; persistence of 6; process of construction 98; role 7–8, 105; understanding of 6–7
mounds 3, 59, 61, 65, 70, 139–40, 144; *see also* long mounds
movement: constraints on by woodland and areas of cultivation 28–9; cycles of grounded in history 39; seasonal 17, 18, 20, 21, 27, 28, 29

Neolithic: definitions 5–6; and Mesolithic 5, 19, 67–8
Norfolk 17
North Stoke 59
Northborough 85, **123**
Notgrove 63
Noyen sur Seine (France) 97
Nutbane 59, **60**
Nympsfield tomb 63, 65

Offham 113, 114, 115, 121, **122**, 141
origin stories 12–13, 21, 31
Orsett 101, 113, **120**, 137, 138

palimpsests 20
Peak Camp 86
Peak District 27, 40, 148
Perryfoot **66**
Piggott, Stuart **84**, 93
pigs 26; eating of pork at feasts 64
pits 29–30, 59, 89, 112, 117
pottery 6, 16, **20**, 29, 68, 116, 128
Pryor, Francis 85, 110, 125

quarries 41, 42, 45, 45–6, **47**, 143

Rackham, Oliver 24
Radley (Oxfordshire) 70, 73
Ramsey (Cambridgeshire) 38
Renfrew, Colin 98–9
rites of passage 21, 28, 31, 60, 61, 118–19
Rivenhall 59
Robin Hood's Ball (Wiltshire) 89, 91, **103**, 139
Roughton 101, **118**, 139
Rybury **79**, 83, 84, 93, 137

Sarup (Denmark) 97–8, **97**
Sawbridgeworth 84
scatters 18, 20, 26, 29, 38, 39, 80;

changes in surface 143–4; and enclosures 91–2
seasons: influence on movement 17, 18, 20, 21, 27, 28, 29; use of enclosures and 92, 93, 100
settlement: and enclosures 85, 88–90, 91–2, 111–12, 138, 141
shamen 63, 64, 73
sheep 26
skulls 119
Smith, Isobel **86**, 93, 117
Snail River pit 15, 29
Somerset Levels 24
South Street (Wiltshire) 61, **64**, 65
Southwick 100, **123**
Spiennes 95
Staines 89, 92, 102, 113, 119, 121, **122**
stock husbandry 16, 27, 40, 92, 100, 104
stone circles 145–6
Stonehenge 147–8
stoneworking 17–18, 19–20, 36–49, 68; ailments suffered while 48–9; and ancestry 48; artefacts taken when leaving site 48; bringing together of people from different communities 40–1, 45, 46, 49; changes in 143; and concepts of identity 39; dangers of working in quarries 44; distinctions made 45, 47; and enclosures 114–15, 125, 126; encountering of past through 47–8, 49–50; and exchange 39, 68; learning of 46–7; mines and quarries 41, 42–4, **47**; organisation of work at mines and quarries 44–6; procurement of stone 20, 36, 37–8, 39, 40, 73; techniques inculcated at sources 49; tool making 6, 15–16, 18, 19–20, 143
Streethouse (Cleveland) 59, **62**
Sweet Track (Somerset) 24, **25**

Tattershall Thorpe (Lincolnshire) 18
Thames Valley 137
Thickthorn Down long barrow 40
Tilley, Chris 158
Tilshead Old Ditch 70
timber: working with 24
tombs 58–67, 69–73, 104, 141; access to 63–4, 70; cattle found in 28, 64; changes in 70–2, 144; closure of 70, 72; distinctions made at 63–4; division of bones 63; earlier Neolithic mortuary sites **62**; endurance of 61; and human remains 58, 60–1, 73; and

kinship 62, 63, 64, 69; linking of communities together 63; linking of sky to land 63; regional differences 59; reworking and embellishment of 59, **66**, 70, 71, 144; rites surrounding 60, 61, 63, 64–5, 119; settings 65–6; ties between present and past 58, 61–2, 65, 66–7; Wayland's Smithy 56–8, **62**

tools: and the dead 123–5; identity and production of 39; stone 6, 15–16, 18, 19–20, 143

Trent valley 40

Trundle, The (Sussex) **100**, 150, **151**

Uffington 85, **118**

Upton **118**

warfare 30, 144

water: as agent of transformation 99

Wayland's Smithy 56–8, **57**, **62**

Weiner, Annette 127

West Kennett **62**, 65

'wetlands' 23–4

Whitegrounds (Yorkshire) 71, **72**

Whitehawk (Sussex) 84, 100, 113, 115, 121, 137, 138

Whitesheet Hill (Wiltshire) 83, **84**, **91**, 139

Willerby Wold 59, **62**

Windmill Hill (Wiltshire) 84, 86, **86**, 88, 89, 114, **133**; deposition 117, **124**, 144; and settlement 99, 115

women 63; burial of 122, 123

woodlands 21–6; clearance of 16, 23, 29, 92; evidence of activities conducted in recent past 24, 26; management of and creation of resources 23–4, 73; role of in people's lives 23

Yarnton 18

Yorkshire coast 40